AF609724

THE AWAKENED

John Stringer

AuthorHouse™ UK Ltd.
500 Avebury Boulevard
Central Milton Keynes, MK9 2BE
www.authorhouse.co.uk
Phone: 08001974150

First published by AuthorHouse 3/28/2011

ISBN: 978-1-4567-7756-2 (sc)
ISBN: 978-1-4567-7757-9 (e)

This book is printed on acid-free paper.

I wish to acknowledge Donna Robinson and my wife Anne for the help they have given me. Also my son Patrick for the painting for the front cover.

THE AWAKENED

The mysteries of the world are far too complex for one to understand in this day and age. Man himself has evolved to a degree that he is not sure of his true self in that which he does and wishes to do. He must start to look inward to see the true self and what he wishes to achieve for himself and the others that surround him. Life is complex and shall always be so for that is the true learning plane that he exists upon. If it was different he would not evolve to that which he must. Man and woman are all spirit and the body that we evolve in is a throwaway thing but it is ones spirit that is important for that is not a throwaway thing and is important in ones development and evolvement of the structure of the universe. For we are all part and parcel of the whole equation and in being so contribute to the betterment of mankind.

Mercies are shown to those who ask; not in the sense of their asking but in the outcome of their asking. Many things seem strange that are sent from the world of spirit but that is not for you to know at this present time. This is why when starting to work with and for spirit the things one receives to give out don't seem to make sense at all. It is sent that way for one is not supposed to know what it is about that one is saying, or giving off for a better term. That is for the recipient themselves to understand and not yourself. We have to work at this understanding of each other for we in spirit have to blend with yourselves for all this to take place and each spirit or person has to be compatible with the soul or spirit that works with you. So have faith in all that you undertake for spirit and see the outcome of one's diligence on the matter. Rome wasn't built in a day as the saying goes and all things that one has to wait for taste better in the long run.

My eyes have seen the glory of the coming of the Lord. He is standing there before us so that we may all observe. His hand is strong and guiding so that we cannot go wrong in the work that we must do and He will never let us down. So look towards your Lord and see what you can envision about that which you think or wish to do. It's up to oneself to decide what one wishes to do; we can only influence one in their own decision. It's up to each individual what they wish to attempt to do, we can only guide one on this pathway of life, but one has to make a start somewhere and from that things can be brought to fruition. So do what you think best and do not be afraid of the attempt. We are always here to guide you in anything that you do or attempt to do.

Happiness is thine sayeth the Lord, happiness in all that you say and do. For to know the Lord or know of the Lord is a great assessment in ones pathway of life that one is travelling at this moment in time. For time is what it is all about; time to live, time to die, time to sow and time to reap. All part and parcel of the great make up of things but not as prominent as of in times past when one had to live by those conditions. Time in one sense has moved onto a different level and the conditions that used to surround one are not there as they used to be. But mankind being what it is adapts as it has done over eternity and shall continue to do so for all eternity. For we are all part of evolution and shall continue to be so until our souls reach a point that this need not take place. That, in the layman's way of thinking, can never take place but be rest-assured that it can and has done so in many instances. Instances that are not attainable for mans intellect at this moment in time but revealed at a later time when one is fully conversant with all that one perceives.

The mysteries of the universe are not revealed to man for his own benefit. Not in his earthly role. For he has to learn to live with himself and those that are around him so that he can adjust in his mind and way of thinking before mysteries as such can be revealed. It's all part of one's survival and learning process that he has to undertake. Man has to understand and explain many things whilst in the physical body for this is needed to compromise his continued existence in this never ending role called life. Life is a beautiful thing in all its extremities and that is how it is and shall always be so for one needs these different extremes to fully understand what truly life is all about. Nature is the same as man himself has found out to his own destruction in some cases. So man has to learn to live and adapt with nature not the other way round as it seems at the moment in the time scale of things. But that is something we all have to learn whether we like to or not. For being what we are we are all part and parcel of the whole equation.

The waves are wringing round the shore for all to see. The sea is a relentless energy. Spirit is the same, for spirit themselves are total energy that is used and dispersed in many shapes and guises. Energy itself is unending and if mankind discovers how to harness this energy fantastic things can be derived from it. Mans progression has been vast in his knowledge on the earth plane and this itself is all part and parcel of evolution. For as it has been said before, without evolution time itself would stand still and things would stagnate and die. Not in the sense that those on the earth plane would realise in their time but it would be a gradual process that would take its toll in many different ways, so we applaud mans achievements and encourage him to continue in his progression. But he himself has to start and readdress things that are happening now for this process to continue unabated. Life is a precious thing and must continue to be so for this in itself is liken unto a garden and the planet we dwell upon is that garden and God in Himself is the owner of that garden and all that are within it. And liken unto today many souls have pets in their domain and this is so with God. So to see species being destroyed is not a happy sight to man himself and God alike. So think on these words for man himself can keep his garden to his own satisfaction likewise can God also. There is wisdom in these words if only mankind can read and understand the underlying threat to us all.

Many things in this world seem mysterious but that is just the makeup of things. If one understood everything that happened to them then there would be no need for examinations and research into the subject for this in itself is what makes man himself unique from all the other species that inhabit this world or planet. Man himself has sought God in all levels of society and has never truly found Him as man and God are all part of the whole equation and when man starts to understand this, things will take on a different aspect to how it is now. We in spirit can only inspire and guide not teach and instruct. It's for man himself to diagnose that which is sent and act accordingly in the way he feels he must do with the information he has procured at hand. The mysteries of life are for oneself to unfold and man being what he is and the integrity inbuilt within him can come up with all sorts of conclusions on exactly the same inspiration or subject. So we in spirit have to attempt to give man the inspiration needed in a form that it cannot be interpreted any other way than the way it is given.

Life is but a series of events that one has to partake in and go through. How one partakes in these events makes one the soul or person that they turn out to be. Life is a gift from God and it can be given and taken away at any given time. One does not know to what lengths one shall abide on this earth plane but the realisation (as you have discovered) that in spirit one continues and are the same when returned from the earth plane puts a different aspect on ones thoughts, for the body that one now emancipates in is like the chrysalis of the butterfly; it is cast aside when its purpose is fulfilled and one again goes to the glory of one's true self. Many souls will not agree or understand these words but do not worry about it; they shall all understand it all one day.

Love rules and conquers all, for without love we are nothing. Love cannot be taught neither can it be taken away. It's part of our inbuilt self. Love comes in many shapes and guises but it is all the same. Those who try to destroy love destroy themselves, for if one cannot give love how can they fully understand the makeup of life itself. We all need love in one form or another for it's through this that makes ones existence palatable. Each soul knows and gives love in a different way and those who profess not to know love have a lot to learn on this pathway of life. Some may not understand from the upbringing that they have encountered but all are open to love if they truly wish it to happen or be so. So take our love and blend it with your love and see the outcome of doing so. For our love is never ending as you one day shall find out.

One cannot simply sit there and expect spirit to give one the answers to that which one seeks. We are part and parcel of the problem that besets us and we ourselves have to come to terms and contend with this problem. No one else can alleviate this situation but oneself. One arrived at this situation through one's own hand for a better word and once in this situation one has to look within oneself to find the remedy to bring this to a conclusion. We are all beset with problems on this pathway of life - it's how we ourselves deal with those problems that make us the person that we really are. As the old saying goes "you cannot have the sunshine without the rain" to understand what the sunshine is really all about. So think closely at what has been said and look towards ones inner self for the answers to these problems. Advice from others is all well and good but one has to put their own house in order.

It all comes to those who wait, for the beauty is in the waiting. Life is full of beauty if one would only look. It can take on many guises and it's up to each individual to interpret that which they themselves see and understand what they have seen. We were given eyes to do this but on a spiritual sense one can see just as clearly but in a different way. It all takes time and training for these things to take place especially so when it has been laid latent for many years. It has to be reawakened and brought to the forefront of one's mind or memory. There are many things stored within one's mind and certain things cannot be brought to the forefront until the time is correct for this to be so. So we in spirit have the task of awakening that which you need at this moment in time. So revel in what has just been shown you and await what else can transpire from one's mind and thoughts.

Tranquillity and peace of mind are a euphoric state of mind to be in. All things are achievable with patience and practice. Nature is a beautiful and dangerous thing; it's just seeing the two sides of it in the right context of things. You yourselves are part and parcel of nature; it's just being able to set one's mind at rest and start to understand it and what it is all about. State of mind plays an important part in how we perceive nature and the things that surround and bombard one on a daily basis. One has to start to see things as through a child's eyes and start to learn what it is all about again. You have done it once so now is the time to endeavour to learn and see it again. For when you look at a child you can see the wonderment in their face when confronted by something new that they have not seen before.

The sky is blue the sea is green

You are both now in between

For this work you have to do

Simply when we think of you

Thoughts you know come from above

Sending you our eternal love

Love that never ever ends

For that is why we are your friends

The family tree is one of divine knowledge and should not be cast asunder. Knowledge is never ending and the thirst for it unquenchable. Knowledge is power, for the more one knows the more one can do in all circumstances of one's evolvement and development. All knowledge is power in the right hands and context of what one wishes to do and gain in both this life and the life eternal. So seek knowledge and absorb all one can on the subject of life, for one shall gain status from doing so.

Possession and possessions are not the end to everything. There is more to life than riches and possessions and we fully understand that one cannot live one's life in this day and age without them; but to possess a vast knowledge of beauty that lies around one is of far greater use when one is finally brought home to spirit again. So start to take in the beauty of nature in all aspect of the word and also other people of different ethnic origins and find the beauty in these people of doing so. You are all spirit enclosed in an earthly body that has to suit the climate and conditions that one is living in. So if we are all spirit, we are all the same without the encumbrance of the human body. Think on these lines and see what you can gain from doing so. It should give you a different aspect to life and humanity as it stands at this moment in time. And yes, we keep on bringing the word time into the equation and it is very important that we do. For time itself rules everything as you will understand at a later date in ones journey through life, but when one reaches that point in time it will be too late to realise what one has missed and what one could have gained if only one had tried to understand what spirit are trying to tell and say, so start to look differently upon life for great things can be achieved from doing so.

Roots of all evil lie in oneself. They fester and multiply. These can be eradicated if given the chance by self analysis and determination. One may grow up with these feelings and traits of character and sometimes be proud of them. They are fools. They feel strong and protected by them and don't give any thought or regard as to how others receive them. All they say is "I am me and that's how I am". If only they would take time to ponder and readjust they would realise the implications of their words and actions. Personal responsibility and free will can often be enemies. Which do you think is more important to the development of your soul?

The magnificence of the universe is there for man to find. It's just a matter of putting mind over matter to start to achieve these thoughts, for this is how it can be translated to those who reach this height of awareness. All things are possible within God's realms and that is infinite. Man strives to attain many things on the material side of life but never puts resources into what might be attained through the power of thought and meditation. Certain countries of your world have this ability and do on a daily basis communicate with the ethos but this must be attuned to the correct bearing on the subject at hand. Spirit have many gifts to give mankind but man himself must be prepared to use them for the benefit of mankind on the whole and not just a certain few who can develop those gifts only for the benefit of themselves. Thought is a very powerful tool in the right hands also in the wrong hands as the world is understanding at this moment in time. So look towards ones thoughts and try to put them to one's own betterment of oneself and those around them. For a kind thought brings all kinds of joy to the recipient to whom it was sent and also the sender of those thoughts.

Death as it is called is only a release from one phase of one's existence to another. We all understand death in one shape or another. It's the after death scenario that most do not understand, and understand those on earth must, to start to learn for the betterment of mankind. Death is synonymous with life; they both go together on ones earthly pathway that one treads to this final ending which is called death. But this in itself is just a beginning of another journey that one continues to walk on this never ending journey. A journey that is eternal in all sense of the word. We live our lives to learn both material and spiritual knowledge that is essential to ones progression on this pathway of life, a life that can only come with a conclusion of our own self assessment of ourselves. One lives to learn and to learn one must live both in the physical and the spiritual also.

Independence in life is all well and good but independence in spirit is no good for one has to blend with those around them to sustain the knowledge of the mass and distribute the knowledge one has gained whilst on the earth plane.

But does one really gain anything by being independent? One lives one's life to attain experience and knowledge and by doing so gives experience and knowledge to those that one touches upon whilst doing so. This applies to both sides of the equation, whilst experiencing one also gives to others that one touches upon whilst doing so. But to try to be independent does, in one sense of the word, limit one's own experiences to what only one themselves wish to know. This in itself helps one to a certain degree but to the overall run of things attains nothing in ones development with others. For learning to live with others is a rudimentary experience that all should try to attain. Trial and error are a great way of doing this, also as the saying goes "never be afraid of making a mistake – the man who never made a mistake never made anything". Great meaning in these words of wisdom, for as one understands without mistakes one attains nothing. Life itself may seem cruel and complex at times but it is all for the good of one's soul. May you try to see life more clearly as you journey down this pathway of life and come to terms with all things that beset one for this is truly what life is all about.

Persecution of the soul is not what spirit is all about. One's own soul sets the standards that one should live and die by. We in spirit are only there as a means to an end. We can only inspire and stand by and watch the outcome of our inspiration. Sometimes it works to our advantage and sometimes it does not, but in all cases it is an experience for the soul to envision. So don't try in oneself to make things happen for happen they will at the appointed time.

Favouritism does not bode well with the world of spirit. God Himself loves all forms of life that is why He placed them there or the means for them to be evolved. So why should He favour one from another? He Himself tries to keep a reign on everything but man being man and having free will and choice in all things makes things very difficult at times. Man himself should learn by past history but he seems not to want to understand this and what it entails, also the knowledge gained from these experiences. This could be understood in time past when man had not the knowledge of the written word, and things had to be stored in one's own mind for the betterment of those around one, but these souls who attempted to store this knowledge might not have had the gift of passing it on and thus took it to spirit with them. The same if one was involved with conflict in one shape or another - man has got to learn for history cannot just be rewritten time upon time again, so look yourself into history and see what you yourself can glean from doing so.

Universal energy is there for all to use but it is the way that it is used that is important. This itself can be used by mankind on the whole but finding out how to use it and to what end it would be used is the difficult question. Man is destroying himself and the planet as it is. To place in his hands a source that makes this easier is not what God and spirit desire, so man himself has to start to make unification amongst each and every creed and breed to find a common ground so that discussions on this subject can be started. Things can be put into place in a short space of time for this to take place but man has first to start to live with himself and nature alike. Spirit are making greater inroads than one can envision for the media does not know and understand everything that happens on this planet at this moment in time and neither shall they until the right person comes along who can pass this information forward without it being distorted for the sake of glorification of the person and media involved. We ourselves are working on this problem and shall and will find a way for this to take place.

Great expectations from the world of spirit do not necessarily mean that one themselves shall receive communication for this source. Things in this world are done for a specific purpose even if at times one does not realise this. We in spirit have guidelines to abide by and those in themselves cannot be breached so one should not automatically think or expect to receive communication from spirit simply by going to a spiritual gathering. We all have our needs to attend to and information will be forthcoming when we feel the recipient needs this information. We hope this does not seem too complicated but that is how things work from our side of the equation.

Simplicity is the key to working with spirit. Do not try to make things complicated just go with what you have got and what you receive. We ourselves have to attune to your own vibrations for this to take place and we ourselves are not infallible so give us some leeway when you are working with and for spirit for it is a two-way thing. We are doing everything possible from our side and it is just a matter of getting the balance correct for it to flow, so do not get discouraged at ones first attempts. We all have to start somewhere and if the vibrations are not correct it makes this all the more difficult. Spirit move in mysterious ways; mysterious to you but not to ourselves, so have patience and always remember that we are always just a thought away, so just ask when we are needed and rest assured we shall help in any way we can, even if in your mind it does not seem so at that particular moment in time.

Unsolicited news is of no use to anyone. Any person at any time can write things and expect others to obey simply because at that time the knowledge of writing was held in the highest esteem. This has always happened and always shall be so. There are always those who will listen and take sides on these utterances, for man has been made this way through giving him choice. Not that that is a bad thing, for without it evolution would not have progressed at the rate it has until now, but man is constantly seeking the truth about evolution and bring into being all kinds of theories that have no true bearing on the subject. God in his entirety understands all things but man has made God many things to many people. So now man kills each other in the name of God and who is this God that they believe and kill for? The self same God as those that are killed believe in! Simply because of writings that have been distorted over eons of time and are still being distorted in this day and age to suit different emissaries of different powers and beliefs. Man himself has got to come to terms with all these different Gods he has created or all shall eventually be lost for man himself and rebirth shall once again have to start.

Withholding information is not what spirit does. It is within yourselves to find and seek the information that you need or seek at that particular moment in time. It is all to do with the simplicity that you have been told about. Your minds are a mine of information just waiting to be brought to the forefront and it's just a matter of sitting and finding out how this information is made available to one at any given time. Time is the key to all things but not the same on the earth plane as in spirit, but with determination and patience this can be achieved. Just remember we are only a thought away and thoughts are powerful things that can be brought into use anytime that one wishes them to, for we are with you at all times. Not necessarily the person who you are thinking about but others who are all on the same wavelength as yourselves, for we ourselves have tasks to perform which one day you will become familiar with and likewise perform these tasks. So have confidence in yourselves and in us and start to look at spirit in a completely different angle for it is simplicity itself when one finally reaches this stage in ones development.

The breath of God breathes within us all and everything we perceive. Take God into your heart and you take the world with you for we are all of the same personage no matter where we live or what we do. We are all brothers and sisters so try to think of all others on this line and start to see how you think and feel about within yourself through doing so. This is one of those simple tasks that we talk about. It costs nothing to do and is well within your capabilities so just try and see what you yourselves come up with and to what conclusions you arrive at. Love conquers all and it always shall do, so as we have pointed out, just try to take the love of God within you.

Visionaries are those who seek or hope to seek the truth of the Lord your God. One can envision Him in many forms and guises, and this is how it has been through the generations of time that man and woman have evolved to at this moment in time. So if God has been portrayed in so many ways, why has not mankind been able to decipher the meaning about all these Gods? Is it just that each sect have their own belief in themselves and cannot and will not take into consideration any others' thoughts and beliefs? For the climax to it all ends the same but with different slants on the subject. So why cannot mankind start to even look along the possibilities of their God being the self same God as all the other Gods that are now in existence for the benefit of mankind? It has taken generations to get man with all his knowledge and technology to this point in time, so why has he not considered the truth and the possibility of it all being the self same God who surrounds us all? Steps must be taken for this knowledge to be brought to the forefront of one's mind before man buries himself to a depth that he cannot resurface from. Words of wisdom that need to be taken heed of.

Anxiety is a natural part of living. We all become anxious at one time or another. It's part of our inbuilt past coming to the forefront of our everyday lives. We need these conditions to help us through our everyday lives; without them things would not be the same and we would not have gained the experience that is needed. That is why so many conditions are placed upon us on this never ending journey through life. Life is what you make it. Some seem to go through life with never a trouble or worry so it seems, but we do not know the underlying truth to that person's makeup and what they themselves have endured for them to have reached that state of wellbeing. We all have our crosses to bear. It's how we bare these crosses that are of the most importance to us and to those who we are concerned with for we ourselves touch upon many souls on our journey through life and how we act and portray ourselves is watched and noticed by others who themselves are influenced in one way or another from this perception. We are part of the animal kingdom and learn in the same format as they do, it's only that our evolution has progressed at a different rate than theirs that we are in the position that we are today. Man himself is quite an intelligent species and shall remain so for the benefit of mankind and all that it encompasses.

"Patience is a virtue, possess it if you can; always in a woman, never in a man" - a verse that could be argued about through eternity, for we tend to put things in the category that suits our needs at that moment in time. One is not given a manual or guide book when one reaches the earth plane, one is sent to make one's own mistakes and to learn from them. How would life be if one had a written conduct that one had to abide by? Not very encouraging one might say, but this is how it is for some souls on the earth plane as it is today and they themselves cannot see past it, for they have obeyed these teachings for so long that they see no other way to interpret life. Like everything else in life change shall come but it must be in a way that is understandable to those who attempt to live their lives in this way and manner. Life is complex and shall always be so for man to try and understand himself. We say man but this is just a terminology on our behalf; woman is included in all aspects of this life on earth and shall always be so.

The wording of things is very important to the world of spirit. How one interprets things that are sent from the realms of spirit is very important for that which is sent to be fully understood. Many a message is not given correctly or not in the right or true context of its sending simply because the medium does not correctly listen or sense what has truly been sent and just makes an assumption as to what they thought they heard or sensed. It's quite a difficult process at first and sometimes even harder when one becomes acquainted with how to interpret, for we all have our own imagination that can and does cut in on these occasions, but with devoted practice this can be eradicated, as you have seen in many mediums. We like to think of them as spirit messengers but one has to be modern in the outlook of things, so 'mediums' has stuck for a better wording.

Visions and inspiration have been sent to many souls over eons of time but these for the most case have been dismissed for lack of evidence. But spirit and your Lord God are attempting to bring evidence to a greater population so that these experiences cannot simply be dismissed by whoever wishes to. Spirit are trying in all parts of this world or planet to bring more souls into the understanding that spirit truly does exist and the final chapter of one's life does ascend and live with those in the world of spirit that have gone before them. People's minds have been set in a divine way for those who wish to believe in what is called a religion; we shall call it this, because of all the religions that now exist on this earth plane at this moment in time. Change has to come but only in a way that it becomes acceptable to all aspects of religion, for as it is at the moment one religion contradicts another and this is where we in spirit are working to bring appeasement to all those souls who have their own beliefs. We understand that it is a difficult subject to talk and even demonstrate upon but this must be so for the benefit of mankind on the whole. Things are instilled into one's mind at an early age and how one wishes to perceive teachings is up to each and every individual themselves, for as we have pointed out we all have choice but as we have expressed many times before, things have got to change for the benefit of mankind today and also in the future, for if it does not, there shall be no future as we understand it at this moment in time. And yes, time is relative in all that we wish to do and attempt to do. One cannot be forced into believing things different to what they have been taught and understand they have to be guided to start to think differently on the subject so that we can influence them.

The world is but a stage and we are the players in a production that never ends whilst one is upon this stage, so one should think that all things are visible to others who surround them and by how you live and by what you do, others judge and make comment. It's the way that you portray yourselves to others that makes you the person you are. This in some instances is difficult for you might feel that why should you worry what others think. "I am me and I shall do what I think and to Hell with the rest of them. I have to live my life and I shall do so as I seem fit". Well this is all well and good but if this form of living is detrimental to the image you wish to convey to people you should stop and think if you want to make an impression upon souls on the earth plane; not in a vanity form but one that makes them think this person is different and seems to know good sense, then you shall have to take stock of how and what you are doing at this moment in time and see if you need to make improvements to your way of living, or in your own opinion you feel justified in how you are portrayed to others. This is just a gentle reminder that what you do and how you act are continuously observed by those on the earth plane and also us in spirit.

Disappointments we all have and shall always have for that is what life is truly all about. You understand that without them life in itself would for a better word become humdrum or boring, for one finds that after one has overcome these disappointments one feels that much better in oneself after having achieved this feeling of wellbeing. Some souls dwell on disappointments and cannot understand why they themselves seem to beset with them. Well it's no good looking to others or blaming others for the condition that is around one at that moment in time, one has to strive themselves to master this affliction themselves and learn from the doing so of it. Many souls rely entirely upon their parents or partners to help solve their problems but the problems are theirs alone and when the parents or partners are taken away, they themselves fall into deep despair.

Happiness comes to those who wait. Many souls seek happiness in all that surrounds them and so in turn try to invent it. If one looks upon this earth plane, there is happiness and sadness all around one; it's just a matter of deciphering each from each other. Many souls themselves bring happiness to this plane without themselves realising it. Nature is one of the most pronounced forms of happiness both for the eye to behold and the soul to distil. Nature is uncomplicated in all its beauty, it's just for the beholder to realise what is there before them for them to start to understand and unravel all that is portrayed. Nature encompasses all the animal kingdom that is there for all to observe but many don't, for they are too blinded by their everyday lives to be able to see and understand these things. Their form of happiness seems to have to be manufactured by man himself thus making it easier for them to indulge themselves in this form of entertainment, for that is truly all it is. Not the true sense of the happiness we are trying to divulge to you.

Happiness in thine sayeth the Lord; whosoever believeth in me shall never die. Dying is not the correct pronunciation for what truly happens. It's just a word that fits the human mind at that time of one's journey through life. We all understand the beginning and the ending of life whilst in the human or physical body. Not many souls understand the implications of what transpires when this cadaver or shell is cast aside. Information has, over the eons of time, been given and sent to those on the earth plane but they have chosen to ignore these teachings and followed their own desired interpretation on the subject, but the time is fast approaching that mankind shall have to take a different outlook on the subject for this planet to evolve as it truly should. Things are coming to a point that there might be no return for those on the earth plane if stock is not taken of what is and has taken place over eons of time. Earth is self rectifying in all aspects of itself but the interference of mankind is bringing this circle to a close. Those who dwell within its confines have to start to understand the complexities of their own existence and the natural and animal side as well, for we are all part and parcel of this great enterprise called life and we all have a part to play.

Everything has its beginnings whether it is on earth or in heaven, for heaven is quite acceptable to those in spirit even though it's a man made thought or word. Our dimension is completely different to your own but runs alongside of yours in the course of your everyday lives. We shall not even try to give you understanding of its existence for it's far too complex for understanding at this given time but we all come to realise its existence with termination of our existence on earth and are then transposed to what you terminate as heaven. Life is to live so do so and learn by all the mistakes and gains that you encompass in this living of one's life. We ourselves have been through exactly what you are now encountering so give us credit that we fully understand your feelings. We ourselves would love to give you more information on this subject but as we have said it's far too complex at this moment in time. That does not mean to say that we shall not be forthcoming with more information at a later time or date. It shall be up to how you develop in the name of spirit, for it would be of no avail to try to teach or show one something that their minds could not grasp.

The visions of the universe are there for all to see and understand, it's just a matter of putting mind over matter to start to comprehend its existence and what it entails. Man has sought from time immemorial to try to understand but so far has failed in his attempts to do so. His thoughts at this moment in time is to attempt to travel to these universal bodies and try to see for himself what and how these celestial forms have been produced. Spirit does not have to be in the human guise so how will those who attempt these expeditions see or understand what is blatantly before them, but not in the way that the physical mind can understand. As we have pointed out before, if and when man can start to use the universal energy that surrounds all parts of the universe then greater insight shall be made available to him and all that it encompasses. Great words of wisdom these, but can or will anyone even try to think on these lines? For that is all man has to do to bring himself into another phase of his existence and gain a greater knowledge of himself and all that he himself encompasses. Think on these things for evolution is all part and parcel of the whole equation. This should give food for thought.

Togetherness is a wonderful feeling and to have togetherness with spirit is awesome. Spirit from the right quarter only come with pure unadulterated love and when this is placed upon one the outcome is instantly known. Spirit come in many different guises thus bringing many different emotions and feelings to the recipient but one has to learn to understand these emotions and feelings.

We all do things in our lives that we wish we had not done but that is all part of our journey through life. Without these experiences how would we learn about the true way of life? Life itself would be truly boring if one had no setbacks. It's when one themselves have conquered or got through these setbacks that the relief and satisfaction that come upon one is great, for that's one more obstacle got over. Many of these obstacles are there simply by one's own devises through trying to attempt something and not sitting down and thinking through exactly what one is trying to attempt. Sometimes one might think that this is not so and that some celestial force has sent this upon oneself through no fault of their own but deep down there is a reason that this condition has been placed upon one. Some never seem to come to terms with what sometimes has happened to them whereas others simply take these conditions in their stride. So try to analyse things when one is beset with problems that one does not seem to understand, for there is an underlying truth to all these conditions and it can be applied to past experiences in most cases.

Guidance only comes to those that seek it. Guidance is often sent and given but to of no avail to the recipient, for often they themselves cannot or will not interpret it. As we have often said and wrote, we can only inspire one in their thoughts, it's how the recipient of this guidance reacts to this inspiration that leads to the final assessment of what's been sent. The same guidance can be given to separate individuals and both can come up with a completely different appraisal. So as we have said many times before, we cannot and will not tell one directly what one should or should not do, it's up to the individual concerned to make their own assessment and act accordingly upon it. It does not seem much of an inspirational message but it's up to the individual concerned to do what they themselves wish to do and we can just follow on behind in a helpful manner. Life is so complex and so it shall always be so for the instrumentation of one's pathway in life and all that it embraces.

Victimisation is not a very pretty word but many souls are involved with such a word in one way and another Many are victims of their own thoughts and deeds whereas others are victims of circumstance which in most cases has nothing to do with them, just the environment that they live in. Some people in some cases love to be a victim of another soul and just live their lives accordingly, but to be a victim of one's own mind is a thing that is most difficult to understand and remedy. We mean this in the sense that outside obtrusion takes place and one is in one sense of the word being controlled by another entity. This in some cases is called schizophrenia and these souls live their lives with this condition until the controller gets fed up or bored with them and releases or leaves them alone. Even then these souls have great difficulty to return to a normal way of life due to the condition that they have been forced to endure for such a long period of time.

You shall learn more on this subject as time goes by, for it's something that spirit wishes to become more aware to the general public, but like all things involving spirit it is a most difficult subject and task to undertake due to all the theories that are being bandied about at the present moment.

Misrepresentation often takes place when working with and for spirit. It's due to communication problems on both sides. We are not infallible and this in itself is ground for things to be misrepresented through communication. This is why one is told to only give what is given and not try to analyse or elaborate on what's been sent, for it's for the recipient to understand not yourselves. You have seen many communicators' work up till now and as you have noticed they all have their own way and style to work with. You must make things quite clear at the outset what standards that you wish to abide by for as souls are on the earth plane so it be so on the spiritual plane and they can be quite frustrating at times, wishing to do their own things but if you set the standards in your first communications then that should prevail whilst one is working with spirit communication. Hope this wording in itself is self explanatory for we cannot put it in any clearer pronunciation. So take heed of what's been said and written and make and abide by your own standards for you will be coerced in different ways, as are the ways with each and every soul in whichever realms they abide in. Always remember we cannot work without you and likewise you cannot work without us, it's just an affable compromise between the two that is needed.

Progressiveness has caused many problems on the earth plane today. Problems that shall take eons of time to rectify, but if man starts to truly realise these problems evolution can still continue on its set course and implementations can be put in place to rectify these problems. We need not go into detail on this subject, for it is far too complex initially to begin with but the media has, for the moment, taken the wakeup call so great inroads can and should be made to counteract that which has already been done and put an end to the continual desecration that is now taking place. We understand that each individual has the right to seek the best for themselves and this also applies to whole nations - nations that have lain dormant and are now wishing to be of the same standard as those around them. This is quite natural but the way in which this can be achieved only puts more pressure on the natural and animal side of the equation, so man has to sit and talk about how these things can take place, taking into account the things that have been plundered from these developing nations for the betterment of these established nations of today. Small things can help in a great way to these nations at this moment in time, for nobody can take anything material into the next phase of their development as was thought in times past. So man, if he wishes so, should set standards that shall go before him when he reaches this next stage of his development. We cannot tell those on the earth plane how to do this, we can only inspire hoping that the inspiration sent is used to good effect. Everybody needs a goal to reach so let's try to make this goal for the good of everybody.

Indecisiveness is the bane of all on the physical plane. You all have so many distractions in this day and age. The things that were common -a –garden events and happenings have now to be thought through before one can in sense get on with one's life, simply because of the effect of what one is doing or going to do might upset some individual who, in your terminology, is streetwise and decides to sue you simply for the money, because life has been turned round to this way of thinking and acting. Not that it would cost the individual any outlay on their part, for in truth they themselves have no compulsion to use what money they have in that way, but simply use the system that is in place to do so. Most of these enterprises have in the outset been instigated to alleviate suffering to certain souls in the community but like all things that are brought into fruition, they are simply manipulated by those of an intellectual mind and used to do things that they were in truth not intended for.

Time is an everlasting and never ending thing. Time is immemorial. We live by time and we die by time, but not in the sense of the word that it denotes on the earth plane. One is simply taken to another dimension where life itself continues. How this happens is too complex to explain so one is left to find out all about it when the time arrives. We all have this process to go through so don't think it is anything untoward. We cannot digress what this side of life is about, all we can say is that it is lovely and *love* being the dominating factor, for the love of your Lord God and those in the spirit realms is something to behold, something we will not even start to explain for the complexities are far from your understanding at this moment in time but time will eventually give and show you this insight which all on the physical plane wish to know about. So live your life to the full and do not be likened to a small child wishing he or she was older and bigger so that they might do things others are doing and they are not allowed to because of their age and size! This is one of the stumbling blocks when being in the physical, for one soon attains these levels that one wished for and then expect to be able or wish to go back to that innocent time again but, as one realises, these things are not possible in the physical sense but can be attained through the mind and all that it has accrued whilst living in the physical. This is why we need to venture onto the earth plane – to gain knowledge and experience for our further advancement in the spiritual sense. We realise that you have had this information before but it is still practical for us to communicate with you and you yourselves with us and as everyone knows, practice makes perfect.

All things come to those who wait and waiting is the operative word. Everybody wants everything now; for this is the way the world seems to want to go. No time for things to evolve in the natural way simply because of the knowledge that man has accrued over the eons of time, bringing him to a stage in his development that seems like a headlong rush to achieve all that he desires in the shortest space of time. We all need time to reflect. Even those in spirit need this but we are not afflicted with the time scale that you live by so things are more acceptable to our way of thinking.

God is our infinite being with whom all things are possible but to just categorise Him is not possible whilst one is still in the physical frame, and why should one wish to know who made God? Do they need this information to try and find some supreme being that could or can be used as some form or kind of deity? All mankind at this moment have their own interpretation of whom and what God is to them. Does not this earth continue to rotate as it does? Does not the waters of the oceans ebb and flow in a regular pattern? Man himself understands these things in his own interpretation of how and why these things occur, so as night follows day why has he got to try and search for something that cannot be understood in this context that he now lives and survives in?

The love of your Lord God is eternal for being part of oneself his love continues with you throughout your existence. We say that life is eternal and that is so but not necessarily in the way you think with the physical mind. One attains a completely different outlook to all things when one reaches the spiritual side of life for it still is life but in a different environment. For as we have pointed out before the spiritual mind is far more complex than the physical one and one shall understand this when this transition actually takes place. As we have pointed out many times before we cannot and will not attempt to try and explain what the spiritual side of life is like but we can tell you in a word that you fully understand and that word is *beautiful*. So until you reach this stage of embodiment we are afraid that this word shall have to suffice for this present time. Also *time* is another operative word that shall and will be understood in the extinction of one's life. Not much to go on one might say but we are afraid that that is all that can be divulged at this moment in time.

Viciousness will always assail the human mind for that was part of mans development in his early survival on the earth plane. It has stood him in good stead in his development through the ages but now seems to be put to the forefront of everything that surrounds him. All things seem to stem from viciousness at this moment in time. Children watch television and games that all encourage this form of entertainment. Life does not have to be this way; it's just that this form of entertainment sells. It is a typical example is likened to Rome in its heyday but it brought them no good because of its corruption. We have to try to turn our attention to other matters and then this inbuilt way of acting and living can be changed for the betterment of mankind, for like attracts like and so the process continues unabated, but we have to make a start at redressing this viciousness and bring a more calming nature to the whole planet. We understand that these things cannot be done overnight but insights should be made in that direction. It's surprising how a small example can be suddenly enlarged upon, for this is how it is with mankind at this moment in time.

Reflections in life are things we always look upon for the guidance and wisdom in the memory of the things that we have done and heard about. Reflections can come in many guises. Some good and some bad but they are all there for the benefit of one's soul, for in truth they are part of our own self assessment and also self judgmental process that has at some time in one's life come to the forefront of our daily experiences. So in hindsight, the more good or nice reflections that one has accrued help outweigh the bad and not so good reflections that one has perpetrated on this pathway of life. At the end of the day though, all these experiences were necessary for ones development. It's how one has come to terms with that which one has done and not done that is the important factor, for if one has not learnt from these experiences what was the point of one's life? That is an overstatement really because everybody learns something on this pathway of life be it bad or good. It's the knowing what is bad in one's own mind and rectifying these examples that one is beset with. It may become hard for some souls to try and extinguish these thoughts and actions that one undertakes. This way of living makes for a profitable existence and to do away with this form of living would seem to bring hardship and loss of respect if one eradicated this from one's life. It's all up to the individual themselves as to what action one might take but be rest assured spirit will always help in these circumstances and bring about another way of doing things.

Disintegration of the world could be an imminent thing if man just continues on the devious pathway of life. Who are we to demand the full attention of those different races, creeds and breeds with all the different aspects of religious beliefs? They all started from one definite point but have evolved into something quite different from that originally intended, but this itself is through man's own interpretation of the subject at hand and his own unique way of thinking on these matters. It's mainly down to the fact that mankind has the power of choice and this shall always be so, for it's the inherent makeup of himself that makes evolvement this way. The timescale of these happenings is not in any lifetime you yourselves can conjure up or understand but seeing as we are the controllers of time it is conceivable that these conditions can prevail. Don't forget though we ourselves are good at inspiring thoughts to the correct sources and persons for this itself to be self governing, but we certainly need mankind to think about mankind on a one to one basis and not on a dog eat dog everyday thesis. Man starts life in all innocence and it's only through the examples set by others that he evolves into that which he is now. This in itself can be rectified with the correct input from the correct souls that do on your earth exist. It's just a matter of bringing these souls to the forefront of our understanding for this to exist. So don't be too alarmed at this knowledge and information, at this moment in time we are just trying to get mankind to help themselves without spirit having to do it in catastrophic ways and, seeing as mankind does not understand time as we do, all we can do is inspire thoughts on this subject and hope it comes up with the conclusion that we anticipated.

"O yea of little faith" sayeth the Lord your God. And that is true in this day and age, for what is faith as the word denotes? Faith is something that we understand to believe in but do not readily know or understand exactly what it is we are believing in. One can have faith in one's ability to do and achieve something, for that itself is self-explanatory, for it has been done and accomplished by oneself but to have faith in a thing that one cannot see or touch is a completely different scenario. Man has this inbuilt strength to help him decide that which he wishes to do and also to believe in. It's all part of our inherent makeup that gives us the driving force for progression and through progression evolution continues to take place, so through one's life examples are set forth and through them one can assimilate that which one wishes to do or pursue. This in itself is how faith exists. Seeing or listening to examples and believing in them, even if one does not fully understand the true implications of it all.

Retribution can come in many ways and not necessarily for one's own benefit. One can be placed in this condition for things one has done and not done during one's pathway of life that they have succeeded to traverse. Not everything is to one's own benefit as it may seem but in hindsight gives one the opportunity to experience these conditions the same as others did due to your own way of living at that particular time in life. It's all part of one's ongoing development in the name of spirit for the experience gained is beneficial to one's own soul. It may at times be very frustrating to kowtow to the demands of others but this is needed to see the broader picture to it all and in doing so gains one the experience to see above these trivialities, for that is truly what they are, but with the physical mind being what it is, it can be blown up into all sorts of complications, each one feeding on the other, so that tit for tat reigns supreme over the whole equation. We hope through this information one can see light at the end of the tunnel, for at the end of the day it's all for one's true benefit. It might not seem so at this moment in time but rest assured it will when this obstacle is surmounted. We work in strange ways don't we? But it's all for one's benefit of one's inner-self that has to emerge as one progresses. I am a spirit not encased in a physical frame and thus see and feel things quite differently to that which you do at this moment in time, but with a little bit of encouragement on our behalf can make great inroads towards solving and helping one's inner-self to start to emerge for that which is needed.

Disposition is a word that could be used in many aspects of spiritual work and also that on the physical plane. One themselves can have a disposition to this, that and all sort of anomalies that beset us on a day-to-day basis. It's how we handle these feelings and experiences that helps us to move forward, for one can quite easily stop in one position and continually mull over certain experiences and never seem to reach a conclusion as to what it is all about, but if one is flexible in one's mind and outlook one can start to ascertain what it is all about and see a conclusion to that subject more easily. This is the advancement of one's mind and spirit. Seeing as they are both linked in kind but with the greater emphasis on the physical i.e., imagination. So when one can start to satisfy one's own imagination that's the starting block to set one off on a great spiritual experience. This does not in fact mean that one shall have no imagination, for that in part would solve nothing in a spiritual sense and physical also. It's just being able to set the harmony between the two that is of great importance to us all. Man and woman are complex beings but not so complex with us at the helm to steer and guide you in the right direction, for this work is liken to being at sea with no points of reference for you to go by, just our influence which is similar to the instruments that the sailors used to take them from one destination to another and if those instruments were used incorrectly they didn't arrive at the designated spot.

Disabilities are not liabilities. We are the liabilities who have to solve how to live and learn with and from that which is thrust upon us. Disabilities come in all shapes and sizes. It does not necessarily have to be a physical one, it can come to one's own mental source making it more difficult for others to comprehend or understand. Just that one does not seem to be conversant to what is happening does not mean that they themselves have no comprehension of what is happening around them. The mind is a marvellous thing and can and does absorb all kinds of things that is thrust upon it, not in the context that those whom to themselves seem normal but to those who others think that there is nothing there and they themselves don't understand anything. This in itself is not true as past experiences have proven, so one should think carefully when dealing with those whose mind one thinks is afflicted, for this is not necessarily so in the understanding that we have at this moment in time. Life is life and life is to be lived even if at times one thinks that some souls themselves have no life. They themselves can be in a completely different dimension to ours even though they are still on the earth plane so do not be too quick to judge others on a face value. You yourself and others cannot read or see the underlying thoughts that that soul may have and he might need this time and condition to understand that which he or she has to learn, so you see - life is much more complex than you ever thought.

Litigation is a word that could be used against each and every country in this world at this moment in time for the things that have been done in the past and also the present. Money now is the dominating force in one's everyday lives. It has to be this way as bartering as of old would be of no avail as things stand today. Man has much to learn and to do so must start to see the underlying signs that are sent from spirit to enable him to do so. We cannot specifically say that which we wish to say for it has to come from man within, otherwise we would be attempting to rule his life and that is not what spirit are all about. We ourselves have had this turn on the wheel of life and now have to stand back and readdress that which we actually did ourselves and seeing as we ourselves made many mistakes, who are we to direct and advise others on the same subject? Evolution is a wonderful thing but the time factor to man is incomprehensible so other ways have to be put in place for this understanding to become reality. We ourselves have to work in a way that is not directly influential to that which we wish to come to fruition. It must be of an inspirational nature that man himself actually brings that which needs to be done into being entirely through his own intervention. Very complex one might say but not as complex as one might think because as we are all spirit in times of need our spiritual side can come to the forefront and help in these discussions.

The anomalies of the mind are there to explore and in doing so will put one on the greatest expedition that has ever been undertaken, for the vastness of the mind is incalculable in all that we understand at this moment in time, for time as we have explained before is of the essence in all things and time is immemorial in all that has been done and all that has to be done. Time controls everything even on a day-to-day basis. One sees fiction both in the written form and also that in the series of films etc that one is inundated with so in fact all things are possible if the correct influences are put in place for such things to happen, but that is up to mankind itself as to whether they wish to explore other regions of the universe before putting in order their own house. For this truly needs to be done in all aspects of the word. Inspiration comes from us and seeing as we are the perpetrators of this inspiration, mankind has to search within itself before we allow this form of enterprise to take place as we are now writing. We are just the lowly souls who do our bidding to enable those on the higher planes to reach conclusions on all that is asked and done on this earth or planet. So you see, we don't see how things can be transposed to those on the physical plane until they themselves put their own house in order. Well that's some new evidence for you to think about and mankind certainly need to think about these things for all things to complement each other.

Personal responsibility is very important in this day and age. Too many people think that everything has to be supplied to them and they themselves do not have to contribute in any way towards how they themselves live and exist. This is one thing that evolution has brought to the forefront of society and is now taken as the norm in certain societies. All have this inborn ability to be the fetcher-gatherer that was of the past but it has been suppressed by those who think that they themselves know better and just pigeonhole people, for they cannot or will not find a solution round the problem at hand at this moment in time. This in itself destroys one's own self respect and forms a new generation of souls who expect to be looked after from cradle to grave, but if some great catastrophic happening occurred it would be surprising how many of those souls would start to find a new self-within-self and start to become self-sufficient in their own eyes again. Life is a complex road that we travel but travel it we must; for all that we need to accrue on the way for knowledge and experience are of great need in all that follows this earthly existence.

Communication is the necessary living tool for every living thing for without it nothing would exist. Communication comes in many different ways depending on the species. It has to be this way otherwise progression and evolution in itself would fail to exist. We all take this for granted, but just try to think how difficult it would be for one race or creed to make contact with another if the different forms of communication could not be portrayed. The same applies to all living things. Not in the sense that one species has to communicate with another but how one particular species can guard themselves against another. This in nature is quite profound, for everything has to have its own living space and be able to defend or warn other species that this space is theirs. Communication with the world of spirit is also significant in this day and age. It is being brought to the forefront of mans mind in certain countries and conditions, so this in turn shall make other creeds and breeds start themselves to take notice and seek information about such things. God moves in mysterious ways His wonders to perform and this has been so down the eons of time, but now communication is on a global nature and news or things can be passed to and fro within seconds, thus breaking down all the barriers that were in place in times gone by. So this is great news for the world of spirit who now can go forward without the hindrances that once existed and it may sound strange but these hindrances come about through that which spirit originally put forth, but man being man thought otherwise and altered the original communication to suit his own needs but put in such a way that it was believed as such.

Condescending is not a word that should be used with spirit. Positivness is more appropriate for without positive thoughts one tends to achieve nothing. We ourselves work on a positive vibration and so should those who wish to work with and for spirit. There are many who have attempted to do this but few who have attained this form of communication simply because they have been sidetracked into trying to do things that are not what spirit actually want them to do at that moment in time. One has to learn the positive way of communication and to do this one must become observant to the things that one is surrounded with. Love and the giving of love are of great importance when working with and for spirit, for in essence that is what spirit truly are. When love is given out most souls reciprocate to it, not necessarily in that instant but sometimes at a later stage when that soul has had time for reflection. And love itself comes in all shapes and sizes so one should practice giving out love and see how others reciprocate to its giving. We understand that some souls that one meets on life's pathway will never seem to be affected by this, but given time and trial things start to form in their thoughts also, even if you yourselves don't see the outcome of it all.

The personalities of the world are varied in thought and deed. It has been ordained so for the accomplishment of each creed and breed to survive, for survival is the main trait of the human soul. It has had to be for the species to survive. In times past things were not as simple as today for technology has played a great part in what we perceive in today's way of thinking and looking at things, but still deep within us all is the survival instinct that cannot be suppressed even after all this time. This in itself makes each and every breed and creed suspicious of one another and the human mind being what and how it is lends credence to these thoughts and feelings. For everybody feels the need for their own personality to survive at all costs. Put this together with others of a like mind and language and you have the perfect scenario for separate societies as they are in this day and age, so for people to become more acceptable to each other these latest barriers have to be broached and truth and light cast upon them for all to see the futility of one's actions in today's society. To do or alter this will take an enormous effort on all concerned but a start has to be made somewhere, for as the saying goes "Rome wasn't built in a day", neither shall the accomplishment of this be so, but as we have pointed out many times before it's just a matter of sowing the right seed on the right ground for this to be brought to fruition.

Deliberation brings consternation to those whom it surrounds, for when one is asked or even inspired to do things, one's mind goes into overdrive and starts to think of all the possibilities that's been asked can conjure up. This is where, in sense, many souls deviate from that which has been asked and make their own interpretation of what it is all about thus bringing consternation to the subject asked in the first place. As it has been said and written many times before, just listen to what's been said and do exactly what has been asked without one's own interpretation on the subject. The giving and receiving messages works in exactly the same way, just listen carefully and relay only and exactly what has been sent through whichever gift is being used at that particular moment in time. This in itself is one of the fundamental lessons of working with and for spirit for your imagination coexists with inspiration. They both work on the same level of vibration but it's up to the individual concerned to understand and decipher exactly what is inspirational and what is not. If one can put themselves in the hands of spirit and truly believe and accept spirit then it makes it all the easier for all parties to become more coherent on the subject and great things can and will be achieved through doing so. Well, it seems that it's back to the classroom again my friends but practice makes perfect and if one does not know exactly what spirit are talking about, how can one avail themselves of this knowledge and understanding? We hope you can grasp what's been said and act accordingly upon what's been sent. You have witnessed mediums that have started giving messages and philosophy only to become bogged down in their interpretation of the subject and seem to go backwards.

To be able to make contact with those in the physical sense is quite enthralling for us. One does not realise the implications of this until one themselves are engrossed in this side of life. We all have our tasks to do but not in a physical way as you understand things. We like you have choice, for in truth we are you without the encumbrance of the human frame. God made a fantastic thing when he made both man and woman. Also all the other forms of life that on this sphere do exist, and exist is the dominant word at this moment in time, for as time itself steps forward, many things are starting to suffer through its course. Souls that populate this sphere or world are all at different stages of development and many of these under-developed creeds and breeds are now beginning to learn about the technology that now exists and through this are finding different ways of life to that which they have always known. This in itself is not a bad thing but in doing so knowledge that has been amassed over eons of time starts to become eradicated and one becomes reliant on the standards in a monitory sense. This is all well and good in some circumstances but when one is beset with conditions that don't exist to bring forth money, then this in itself alters the whole strategy of what it is all about, for this in turn puts great pressure on the animal and plant kingdoms, and kingdoms are truly what they are in their own sense of the word.

Suffer little children to come to me and forbid them not for such is the kingdom of Heaven. We write Heaven as it is the easiest way of explaining one plane from another. Everything has to be called something for one to start to understand what one is talking about. In times past things had to be given in storylines because most people could not read or write and this was to be so for generations until the written word came to these different tribes and breeds as they were classed at that moment in time. Now due to the written word the majority of souls on this earth can understand and use the written word so the need for things to be told in storylines need not be given, but in truth all that spirit send to those at services and circles is still in the form of speech and this in itself can be distorted for the benefit of those relaying the actual message from spirit. We keep emphasising this about just giving what you receive and this is perfectly true. How do you think spirit themselves feel after they have made the effort to come to their loved ones with information that they themselves feel is relevant at that moment in time only to find that the soul who is relaying this message starts to try to interpret what's been said themselves and put a completely different twist to the message? How would you yourself feel if this happened to you and you could not do anything about it, only to stop the inspiration when one wanted to give more? So you see it's of the greatest importance to only give what you get even if it means absolute nonsense to oneself, there is a reason behind it all. We hope you do not feel that we are overemphasising what we are trying to put over to you but there is a very good reason that this should be so and you will benefit from listening to what has been said.

Inconsistencies are allowed in one's development for no-one is perfect. And what is perfect? If one was at all that way one would not be their true self but just an automaton of spirit doing exactly what one was inspired to do with no input from one's own intelligence or intellect. This is why one's imagination plays such a great part in one's everyday life, for imagination and inspiration are on the same level and vibration thus assisting us in the world of spirit to inspire one's thoughts and bring fresh knowledge to each and everyone. Don't think for one moment that you are just run by spirit through the thoughts that you get. Your imagination is a powerful thing and also your inner-self, which at times comes to the fore also giving you information that you need. Some souls, as you have seen, are more attuned to inspiration than others. This is simply because they themselves have taken the time and effort to make this so. We all have to live our lives to the best of our ability and in doing so gain experience and knowledge. It's how we interpret this knowledge and experience that makes the difference from one soul to another. Each has their own role to play in this game of life and how one plays this game is the main factor in what one achieves from doing so. So seeing as we are all different in size, shape, colour etc we likewise are inspired differently thus making for different ways of working through our everyday lives and also those who are inspired by spirit, making each and every one different in their way of working and thoughts on the matter. We hope this tries to give you a greater insight as to how things work with and through spirit, for at the end of the day we are all individual and to find one in spirit to match is no easy task, but it does get accomplished as you have seen for yourselves.

Today's a good day to write so let us begin. The world is full of all kinds of souls who wish for all kinds of things. We ourselves have been in this self same position and can relate with everything one thinks and wishes to do, but one must think carefully as to what one wishes in some instances, for not all can be forthcoming in the way that we ask it, otherwise what would be the point of life if one just asked and one received to their heart's desire? Everything has to be earned (in one sense of the word) just the same on the earth plane as that in the higher side of life, for without this carrot and donkey attitude nothing would work in the true sense of things, for some of the things that some souls ask for are quite extraordinary. We shall not give examples but we are sure that your mind can comprehend such asking, and in one sense, what is the point of asking for something that you yourselves caused to be altered when in fact you yourselves were the perpetrators of the question asked? Love is strange. Many people take it for a game as the song denotes but this is perfectly true. Many souls have the love of others and cannot and will not see it simply because they themselves are incapable of giving and returning love in their way of thinking but this is not so, for all souls are capable of giving and receiving love, it's just a matter of trying to do so with and when the conditions that surround and assail them seem to make this form of communication impossible. God Himself is true and never ending love and to walk with God is an amazing and beautiful thing to behold but many do not see it this way, for they think that because God is part and parcel of everything that surrounds one that He Himself is responsible for that which assails one in their everyday lives. They do not think or imagine that they themselves could be part and parcel of the scenario that affects them at that moment in time and have been placed in that position to see how they themselves react to the conditions around them. This is some instances may seem cruel to some souls but that is how life is for one to gain the experience that is needed for one's progression. One might say that this is wrong in some instances but one does not know what that soul originally asked for before being sent down to the earth plane, so just think on these words of wisdom before judging or condemning others.

The spice of life shall always be here for all eternity

As down this road you seem to pass, thinking thoughts that do alas

Tell you things you wish to know, that we shall always love you so.

So walk this walk and you will find, the answers to things that's on your mind

We're here to help you as you go, even if it may seem slow.

There's need for it to be this way and we will show you one fine day.

So carry on as you must do, for you need us as we need you

To do this work that lies ahead, even if you sometimes dread

The time it takes to make it so, as down this pathway you both must go.

Rome wasn't built in a day my friend but we will be with you to the end

In all you do or attempt to do, for all our love is always true

To those who help us as we pass, along this road that leads to grass

To ease our feet as we must tread, the endless road that lies ahead.

So goodbye for now and just take heart, for at this moment we have to part

And start again and you will see just how easy it all will be.

Inconsistencies in life attain and avail nothing in the true sense of the word. Positivisness attains all things if used correctly and by this we mean in thought, word and deed. Many can attempt many things but few achieve what they originally wanted through being diverted onto different courses through life simply because they themselves thought that this other way was simpler and easier. Nothing is given to anyone. One has to earn the privilege of attaining certain things in life and thus it is so when one starts to attempt to do something and does not complete that task, one is laying the foundations as to how one shall live their earthbound existence. We live by who we are and that is what all souls need to understand, for if they did the difference to their lives would be enormous. This does not mean that if one at first does not succeed in what they are first attempting, that it shall be liken this through all their lives. If one starts to realise that what they tried to do did not succeed through their own incompetence, then they are on a new foundation or beginning. Life is all trial and error; it's knowing the difference between the two that makes the difference from one soul to another, for one soul can learn from another just as one did from one's own parents whilst young. This still applies when one has grown older, for one never stops learning and one can still be amazed at things that one sees and learns from even at a great age in one's pathway of life, it's just that one did not see the relevance when it was shown at an earlier time, even though they themselves wished to know of such things, so my friends - life is a never ending story, it's just that sometimes one is paying attention to what's been told or shown at a particular time and thus learns from it.

Intolerance to others thoughts, words and deeds is definitely not tolerated when working with and for spirit. One has to try to see the reason why that soul acts in such a way as to make them seem intolerant to oneself. We all have standards to work by. Many of these standards being ingrained from our parents and those that have surrounded and touched upon us as we have walked this pathway of life. One has never run in the circumstantial evidence of one's pathway, one has always walked and it's through this manner or method that one has learned and accrued such thoughts and emotions whilst doing so. This also applies to those whom, at times, cannot understand the reasoning for their attitude and way of life. Well, seeing as you have not lived their life and all that it has contained, who are you or anyone else to judge such souls? We all walk a pathway that is there for us, it's the obstacles that are put in ones way that denotes how and why we react in the way we do that in fact can alienate one to others. Each and every person is an individual, all having their own foibles to contend with and in some circumstances making one unacceptable to others, so one should not be too judgemental of others because one's own way of living and acting can in itself be quite alienating to those whom you are being judgmental about, so try to start to look upon others with a more rudimentary view and see if through doing so, one can find an excuse for their being that way in the first place. It would avail nothing if we all had the same thoughts and concepts in life, for what would one actually achieve through being that way?

Experience of life, love, good, bad etc., are the greatest learners of knowledge for one's soul and mind. In one's life on the earth plane one attains many experiences which, in many cases, makes us stand back or sit up to what is happening to us. It's through this medium that we learn everything that needs to be known. One can attain knowledge from books and other souls but to truly interact with an experience stamps that knowledge within our very being, making us actually take note of such experiences. Most life that we know about learns from doing so. There are many forms of life that have an inbuilt form of survival but still need to do things to experience this inbuilt form of living. Life is one great big experience on a day-to-day basis and it's how we react with that which is thrust upon us that makes us the person that we are. Many souls experience many things but do not seem to learn from doing so and continually find themselves placed in a situation time and time again, but seeing as everyone has choice in all that they do to a certain degree, who are we to say what they keep doing in our way of thinking is not correct but must seem correct in their way of thinking, for we all have different goals to try to achieve and what might suit one soul certainly would not suit another simply because of how and where that soul started his or her life experiences. So go and experience all one can, be it good or bad, for all experience is knowledge and knowledge is the most powerful tool that one can attain, for without knowledge and the capability of storing that knowledge, mankind and all the other species that can accrue such things would certainly not have been able to survive until this moment in time.

Everything in life is and has a season; a season to live and a season to die - it's all that lies between that is of the greatest importance. We all perceive different aspects on our journey through life. It's how we react to these different aspects that make us the person that we are. Life and the love of life have to be lived to the full. It's also how we ourselves perceive the meaning of full. It means different things to different souls so no one actually sees things in the same light. One should never see life as boring, one should be able to see beyond the obvious and reach a conclusion that suits one's own intellect, for we are in fact quite intellectual in all aspects of life, it's just our ability to bring it to the fore that stands in our way many times. Things are learned at an early age from one's parents and loved ones and this in itself can cloud one's vision as to the true aspect of what one is actually experiencing, simply because others that you have learned from could not themselves grasp what it was all about, but you have us to inspire and guide you in all that you do or attempt to do. So start to look upon life in a different vein, for there's more than meets the eye if one would only try to see and absorb these happenings. We can only place these things before you if you are in the correct position for such things to take place.

The world is a stage and mankind and all that dwell upon this world are the actors, so one must think that all that is done is seen by someone, maybe not in the physical but certainly in the spiritual sense, for seeing as we are all linked, things themselves can be felt in the spiritual sense during their conception. Some souls have these sightings or premonitions of things to come during their physical sense. Many don't understand this phenomenon but be that as it may, this does occur. The animal kingdom has its own way of adapting but this is being made harder and harder through man's intervention on its habitat, but time will tell my friends as to how far this trend shall be allowed to continue, for the world stands at a great pinnacle of its evolvement and the pros and cons of its evolution have to be looked upon in greater detail, so let's hope that man himself starts to look upon himself and see if he can readdress this situation that he now lives in. God and spirit are making great efforts to bring attention to these matters but at the moment to no avail, so we are at a stage of impasse and have to await the outcome of divine intervention. Not very happy thoughts but we shall have to see how these things can be adjusted for the benefit of all.

When working with and for spirit it is of the greatest importance that one understands that one is truly working with spirit and accordingly adapts the correct procedure for this to take place. One has to open up to spirit and by this we mean that one automatically has a spiritual sense but it's not that that needs awakening, for it's always there. It's one's physical sense that needs to give one's spiritual sense the permission to go forward, to be able, without any sense of guilt on its part that it is intruding upon one's own physical sense and this in itself is quite simple to achieve, for all one has to do is to make the true commitment by and through opening up to spirit and all that that entails. Each and every soul has its own way of doing this exercise; for that is precisely what it is, an exercise in one's commitment to release one's spiritual from and with one's physical, so that no intrusion takes place from either side, for once one is in this state of wellbeing we spirit have full rein on the matters at hand and can work accordingly with that which is needed at that moment in time. Very complex, one might say, in the explanation of it all, but quite simple in its operation.

Blessed are those that worship the Lord for theirs shall be the kingdom of Heaven. A euphemism in one way of talking, but a complete truth in another. We all have our own conception of what we believe Heaven is all about. We say Heaven, for that is a nice way of putting it and it has been this way since the written word was established, so why alter it for some modern intellectual slang? Whilst in the physical form it's hard to even try to comprehend how all this takes place but those on the earth plane are starting to understand that there is another dimension which is involved and intertwined within the physical plane. More information is needed on this subject for those of the mass media to try and understand and this in itself is where we in spirit come to the forefront of the equation, for it's through the likes of yourselves and others in a similar frame of mind that we in spirit can start to try and influence a greater audience. There is certainly a much greater interest and involvement in the media on this subject at this moment in time and that is truly what we in spirit need to happen. We ourselves cannot simply step forward and say "here we are; now you must believe". That is no good. It has to be through a gradual understanding for mankind to try to take this on board. There are generations of souls and their history that lies behind them to be overcome and understanding of it all to be portrayed in a manner acceptable to all those who are involved in their own understanding of what in fact happens to those that have died in a physical terminology. We can only divulge certain information over a period of time for this in itself to be understood and taken on board.

Consideration on all aspects of life is a great asset when working with and for spirit, but to apply such consideration takes time and effort on any who wish to attain this level of commitment. Working with and for spirit is not as easy as one thinks simply because of all the complexities involved. It's like expecting somebody to do something with no plan or drawing and no one to ask and no one to see, but to simply sit and trust in one's own self with one's imagination as well and expect that when one does sit, that those from spirit shall step forward and give one the inspiration that is needed. So you see, it is all down to trust. Trust in yourself that this is possible and trust in us to bring the inspiration and evidence needed for such work. Think of the impact en-mass if spirit need to implement some condition upon the planet, for spirit quite outnumber any figure one could amass and just think of the power they could bring to bear on any given subject if the need was there. This is why spirit are making such inroads toward the earth plane to try to make mankind try to understand that there is more to life than meets the eye at any given time and with all this power what can be achieved for mankind itself if only mankind would begin to understand and listen.

Every journey has a beginning and an ending if one wishes it to. We all live in a world that we truly don't understand and by understand we mean the complexities that make this world tick. This world in itself is enmeshed and intertwined with the world of sprit and the universe itself and when you take these things into context things in one's mind become complicated, for there are so many different traits of thought on the subject that no one seems to understand the underlying thread to it all and arguments and discussions become quite profound when these subjects are broached simply because no individual has an in-depth knowledge of all these happenings, so consequently nothing can be resolved. Spirit have a great task ahead of them. A task that is complicated in itself because of all the different religious beliefs that each and every one at some stage in life believes. Spirit are not a belief, they are a true fact which can be proven without doubt but in doing so would cause all kinds of complications.

"Little words of kindness, nothing do they cost, but when they are missing, life's best charm is lost". Perfectly true words in all sense of the words that they portray. Kindness is one of the easiest qualities to portray to others but so often lost in the everyday run of life. Kindness can be shown in so many ways too numerous to mention but to actually portray kindness to others seems, at this moment in time, quite lacking. Life, one finds, is very complex in the respect that one has often shown kindness to a soul only to have this kindness thrown back in one's face, but do we really know why this happened and was it really meant that way or was it just how we ourselves interpreted this action? For, really we do not know what's going on in other's minds in a time like this. Was it just that that soul did not know how to accept such a thing in this way? Or was it just that this kind of act had been presented to them before only to bring them hurt in some way, and at the bottom of it all did that soul, on reflection, wonder why this happened? And in itself gave them a different insight as to how to approach such a thing if it happened again; for time to think about things is a great healer and that what was given freely could, in this case, bring understanding to that soul. When taken into that context who are we to judge others on their outward appearance towards others?

Inspiration is a wonderful thing if collected and interpreted in the correct way. This in itself is the secret to all communication with the spiritual side of life. This has been done through eons of time for the benefit of mankind. It has also led many to dangerous situations as history itself has proven, but with today's technology and general understanding of things makes this kind of communication easier to accept. Many souls of different creeds and breeds have this same form of communication but do not advertise it as it is done in the western world, but we in spirit are making great inroads in that direction to bring forward these souls who have this ability to be more open in their knowledge of such things. Time and tide waits for no man and likewise so with spirit, for the time is now of the essence for such knowledge to be brought to the forefront of all mankind for the true benefit of all mankind.

Holy Ministers of light hidden from our mortal sight but whose presence can impart peace and comfort to the heart. We all need peace and comfort in one way or another in this hectic lifestyle that one tends to live in. Peace and comfort can be attained in many different ways if one would only search for this inner peace that is available to all asunder. This may sound simple and quite straight forward but to actually find and do this simple task is quite difficult in today's society. When young, we had no such inhibitions as we have today. Our body and mind was young and eager to learn anything that was thrust in our way. We went to places that we should not have gone just to see what was there and the reason why we were told not to, but when one becomes older and sees life through a different pair of eyes, one becomes set in ones ways and has not that childlike sense of adventure that used to beset one. This is one of the secrets of finding inner peace and comfort to be able to switch off and go and do things that are not part and parcel of everyday life. Within this realm, not of fantasy but of a different nature, one starts to see things in a different perspective and this in turn gives one food for thought. One need not go to extremes in this way of thinking, just try going around one's own domain in a completely different way or direction and see the outcome of doing so.

Insignificant is the human form in the overall run of life. Man as one species is having a dominant effect over all other species on this earth and in doing so is bringing great hardship to many other species. This in itself has to be rectified and seeing as all species are part and parcel of God, why should God in His infinite wisdom let one species overrule all others just for the betterment of themselves? This is a question mankind has to look into, for if he does not what's to say that God shall let this form of intrusion continue? Everything has been placed upon this planet for a purpose and that is evolvement of each and every single species over a time scale that the human mind cannot seem to grasp. God moves in mysterious ways His wonders to perform and mankind will have to be awakened as to this assumption that all is correct doing what mankind is doing. A readdress needs to be implemented before things get to the stage that species shall disappear, all for the dominance of mankind. Man should look carefully on this subject and see if he himself would be in agreement if some other species became a dominant force threatening mankind. Would mankind agree that this should be so with their own survival put in jeopardy?

Transition comes to us all. It's how we perceive transition that makes the difference from one soul to another. There are many souls of different creeds and breeds on your earth plane and, with being this way, all have different beliefs as to what God Himself is truly all about, so, as we have said, that transition has to take place in the framework of their beliefs otherwise how would one know what to understand at this point in one's pathway of life. For seeing as the life that one has understood up until that moment has seemingly ended, how is one to understand what in fact has actually happened? It's a thing that happens to us all and many souls find it hard to accept but great inroads are being made in that direction simply through the media attention that is taking place.

Being passionate whilst working with and for spirit is not a bad thing. It's how one portrays that passion that makes the difference between one soul and another.

Many people are passionate about what they do and believe and there is nothing wrong with that until, in some cases, it is taken to the extreme. We all have to evaluate that which we are doing and where it is leading us. Some souls just follow a lost cause simply because they will not listen and cannot see beyond that which they think they already know. It's the art of believing in something and still being able to listen to what others say about the matter that makes the difference between believing and being obsessed. We hope you can read between the lines in this information, for it could and can apply to many souls. Being in this frame of mind makes it difficult for spirit to help one to move forward to that which one is needed to do. As we have pointed out, inspiration is only as good as one's mind on the subject, for seeing as one's imagination can play a great part in one's everyday occurrence makes it most difficult for inspiration to get a foothold.

"Blessed are the peacemakers, for they shall inherit the earth". These are simple words but with great meaning. If only mankind could start to envisage the implications of these words great steps forward could be made. Monetary values are needed in this world today but not in the way that it is distributed at this moment in time. Mankind knows full well that what is happening to the natural side of life is not sustainable and many things shall and will be lost forever, so this is why spiritualism needs a full step forward to rectify that which is happening, for if this happens other religions shall have to take note and they themselves start to comprehend. Everyone is capable of influencing this kind of thought and if enough start to think this way, things will start to change for the betterment of mankind. We understand that we keep on beating the same old drum but it must be done to alleviate the suffering to the earth. It's only this that sustains you all and without it mankind has nothing at all, so continue your own appraisal be it only small in your estimation but with others of a like mind putting forth their own input, amazing things can start from such happenings.

Insecurity comes to everyone. It's all part of life's traits. We need the feeling of insecurity to make us look at life in a different manner or way. To feel secure is all well and good but nothing lasts forever and insecurity sits within that same framework, for it's all part of one's learning in this world that one now abides in. When one has to look for an answer to things that surround one, it's then that one is learning for future reference. Many things assail one on this pathway of life and it's through these experiences that one finds progression. It's no good just asking another soul for the answer, one has to live that experience to get that answer for oneself and each and every trial and tribulation is different for every soul otherwise evolution would not progress as it should do. We need these experiences for the good of our soul, for it's that which survives through our transition to our next phase of our journey through eternity.

Independence in mind and body is a stage everyone wishes to achieve. Independence of the mind can be achieved but to do so one has to be able to control one's own imagination and that in itself is a very difficult thing to do and achieve. Many different tribes or souls have in past times achieved such a state of embodiment but things were on a different level to what they are today, but with endurance and dedication such a state of wellbeing can be achieved. To be independent of the body is quite another task because of the way one lives. The nourishment one consumes in this day and age works against one. In times past one had the correct food and different formulas to help keep the body correct. Whereas today one has the technology to overcome all kinds of illnesses but not always in a way that is beneficial to the body itself, so as you can see, in times past the knowledge was there but not the technology and likewise the food was there but not in the variation that it is today.

Blessed are the faithful even when they are perpetrated upon for that is the will of the Lord. Many people are faithful to many things and have been so over eons of time, but to have faith when persecuted for that faith shows true identity in that person. These things have happened all through history and not just in a religious format. Many souls have had beliefs and have carried them forwards even when such beliefs were persecuted. Today many souls look upon things differently simply because of the knowledge that has been attained, but this does not necessarily mean that they are right in their thoughts. Knowledge is a precious thing that is often wasted in this day and age. There is knowledge stored in various ways from the past that could be used to good stead. We have pointed out before these things are not easily available to the public in general, so such knowledge is lost to the world on a whole, but one in spirit is capable of bringing forth such knowledge again, for it was us initially who gained it and put such knowledge to pen and paper.

Writings and words alter over eons of time as does life. Evolution is on a time scale that the human mind cannot comprehend and so it shall always be so, so those who contend to be versed and be knowledgeable about such things have far to go to be in that category, but being as no one knows the true answers to such questions and queries they are revered by others hoping to gain such knowledge. This is part of the human life; always striving to find answers to the questions. Well, that in itself is part of evolution and the questing mind of those that dwell on the earth plane. Many different souls have written many different things about what has happened but nobody seems to take notice and others bring forth new theories on such subjects and the old works are put to one side and not used as they should be.

Blessed are the ways of the Lord and all who follow them. Now this might sound unconvincing in the manner that it is said, for what guidelines have one to go by? Well, you have your own appointed laws and also you have your own inbuilt conscience to guide you in that which you should and should not do. Now as each individual is completely different, each shall have their own assumptions as to what these ways may be. It has to be this way to encompass all the different souls that upon this earth do dwell. Guidance has been given in times past but this became outdated as man himself evolved thus causing more things available to him and so interpretations were set down as to what should be and what should not be and this, through the eons of time and the interference of those in power, brings to how we are at this moment in time, with one race killing another all in the name of your Lord God. This cannot be right in any sense of the word and we in spirit are now working upon a solution to try to rectify these things. Deep are the mysteries of the Lord your God and all those in spirit also, for we are as a team set up and working towards a goal that one day shall be reached and then great revelations shall be made to all asunder.

People often sit and stare, thinking their lives are going nowhere

But as I sit and write my son, you will find what needs to be done

It won't take long as you will see, if you only think of me

I am the one who's gone before, so I can meet you at the door.

The door that you must go right through, to find out what you must do

It won't take long as you will find, when I come into your mind

A mind that's full of thoughts right now, but I will teach you what to do

It does not rhyme you seem to say, but will be clear to you one day.

A day that's very near right now, and then I'll show you how

To do the things we wish to be done, for we do treat you as our son

We know you are and so do you, every time we think of you

So take our blessings as you may, and we will help you day to day

To learn and do what you must do, even when we think of you

So just relax and let it flow, as down this pathway you must go.

It's straight and narrow as you will find, when you bring us to your mind

A mind that's full of doubt right now, but do not worry, we will show you how

To do the things we have in mind, and everything you find will be kind.

The kind we mean will always be, when you start to think of me

Who are you then? You seem to say, but you will know me soon one day

A day that's very near right now, and then I'll start to teach you how

To do and know what you must know, as down your pathway you must go

Not on your own but with Anne too, for both to learn what you must do

We keep repeating these words you say, but it's just to help you day to day

So you don't think you're on your own, as you start to learn what's going to be shown

In different ways as you now understand, and everything shall work out grand

You're doing well so don't give in, in this world so full of sin

It might not seem so to you right now, but we will teach you as from now

To take on board what you need to know, as down your pathway you both must go

To reach for us the appointed place, and you can meet us face to face

We do not mean when you have passed in life itself, for that is sitting on a shelf

Full of dust so we let it be, until one day you both shall see

The dust has gone and you shall see, all you need when you think of me

I'm quite a problem on your mind, but you will find I am quite kind

To those I love from day to day, so try to think of me I pray.

Man and woman are wonderful beings in all sense of the word. Likewise all living things on this earth, be it in water or on land, they are all unique in themselves. The plant life of this planet evolves in its own fashion and will always do so. Things come and things go. We all have a time to act and play in this circle of life and how we perform such acts is up to each individual themselves and in doing so this in itself denotes how other species of all kinds evolve and survive. So all in all, man plays a great part in the evolvement of this planet and should be responsible for that which happens during his stay on it. Some people are starting to realise this and are trying to bring forth some kinds of resources to combat what is happening but this is just a stepping stone to that which needs to be done. As one understands, nothing lasts forever, only God Himself, for He is eternal and that we cannot understand in the timescale of its evolvement, so let mankind start to awaken to what's around them and see what they can do to alleviate such conditions, for they themselves brought about the way things are.

Individuality plays an important part when working with and for spirit. We in spirit are all individuals but all part of the great scope of things so it is so with those that are now in the physical sense, for we are all connected. We put it that way so we don't have to make great complicated explanations as to what it is all about. It's a very difficult task trying to explain to souls that everything and everyone are all connected in the spiritual sense of things. It's difficult enough to try to tell souls or people about the world of spirit because of the way they have been taught and brought up in the world of the physical being. Everybody learns from their parents or those close to them at an early age and one progresses in life through what they see and what they encounter, so one can understand the misconception that one has about spirit or ghosts through all the media attention and all the pictures and story books that are written upon the subject.

Many souls search for perfection in their everyday lives, be it the work they do, the lifestyle they live or the hobbies they pursue. What is perfection? Is there any book or written records of what perfection should be or is it just within the human mind of what they think it should be? And who are these souls who reckon on what perfection should be in all the different scenarios that exist today? To attain perfection in any given subject is not without its complications, for one finds that once one soul has conquered one stage in the game they are playing or working upon, others bring forth other information and skills never even contemplated. It's a continuous, never ending journey with the goals open at both ends.

Compassion is a wonderful word full of meaning if one really thinks about it. Everyone feels compassion at some time in their life and in doing so helps the soul that they were thinking about. We all need these feelings at some time in our lives. Grief plays an important part, also it is a way of bringing one release from feelings that one does not truly understand. For humans, the mind is a very complex machine and can conjure up all sorts of scenarios to any given subject, but when grief comes to the forefront it helps one to release emotions that lie within oneself for the betterment of oneself, for it is all part and parcel of this journey through life that one has undertaken to do. This goes down to experience and experience and knowledge is truly what life is all about because these are the only commodities that one can take with them onto the next stage of development of one's soul. We say soul as some would not agree with the termination 'spirit' in the way many have been taught to believe and whatever they believe is correct for them, for we all end up as it were in the same place and it's then one starts to fully understand oneself and those around them. We live our lives on the earth plane as we think best. There is no book to show us what to do, we learn by example and experience.

Better things have been asked by those gone before but did they solve anything? We all have our own expectations from this life we are living and sometimes cannot seem to live up to or overcome these expectations. That is simply because we do not fully understand how or what these expectations will turn out like. We all have visualisation in our minds eye of what we expect but sometimes the reality is not actually what we expected. Quite complex wording one might say but the best we can contribute at this moment in time. Life teaches us many things as we travel along this pathway of life. You have to live your lives in the circumstances that surround you, and how you live your lives is entirely up to oneself. We in spirit on the other hand have already experienced the physical form and the conditions that it places upon one, so to stand back and watch others go through similar experiences and not in fact give direct help and information on the subject at hand is quite frustrating at times, but we can inspire to a certain degree whether this inspiration is understood is a different matter, for all experiences are different in their entirety. You have the information on a global scale at your fingertips through the media attention that surrounds you day to day - quite different to many of those souls now in spirit.

Retribution is a savage word but not in the context of some of its uses. An eye for an eye works in some instances but not overall. Everyone has done things they wish they had never done but that's life. In life we experience many things that upset and hurt us, it's the response that is important to us. We all have an inbuilt sense of defence, so that whatever is done to one, one can react in the same instance to protect oneself. Love is the KEY to all. Love conquers everything. If the whole population of the world could learn this it would be self-evident to each and every soul, but there are many souls who have never had the feeling of love and they have underlying thoughts that are deeply imbedded within themselves.

Principles are all well and good if one can abide and live up to them. We all set ourselves principles that in some instances are too high for our way of living thus causing all kinds of consternation to ourselves and those around us. One would say that the old terms of life were easier but this is not necessarily so, for we ourselves were involved in those eras and we found it just the same as yourselves, so the secret really in life is not to set your sights too high, then, when you feel you have achieved that level of improvement, one can then look forward to ones next accomplishment, being careful not to try to advance too rapidly. One will then find things can be accomplished much easier. Everybody wants to advance oneself, for that is the make-up of the physical being but to do so makes great complications in some instances. Debt is easy to come by and has always been the same. If one can live at the level they are at and be happy and comfortable with what they have then that makes the difference for a happy and peaceful life. It seems everybody wants the best of everything and the only way this seems to be accomplished is by force and strength and if it starts by showing a standard of force and strength, one has to constantly live up to these standards to enforce them, so conflict starts and once started is hard to call a stop without losing face.

"Peace on earth, goodwill to men". Words recorded in times past and also with many other writings or scriptures. Man himself in many cases has ceased to understand and take note of such writings. With many religions it's just a continuous referral to what has been written in the past with an up-do-date emphasis put upon it. Spiritualism has a completely different approach in the guise of philosophy that is given at services around the world. More emphasis needs to be given to philosophy because that is one time when spirit can truly take over and give in fact true information, if the medium concerned is willing to go down that pathway. Some mediums are afraid of such control, thinking it might have repercussions upon themselves and who they are actually working with. We in spirit understand their concerns and try to give encouragement to those concerned but it seems like another great struggle for mankind to overcome.

Opportunities are portrayed to everyone. Many see or think they see them but do not react in a positive way at that moment in time. That's why many times things are portrayed and one thinks about them and then later decides to go with what's been portrayed only to find some other soul has taken the opportunity and done what you then wished to do. Not, we might say, in the same context as you would do, but never-the-less has taken the opportunity or the bull by the horns and made forward progression. How many times in one's lifetime has this happened, even from a young age? So as you see and as the old saying goes, 'strike whilst the iron's hot'. The mind and thoughts are very powerful things even if you do not realise it. Thoughts, in one sense, are living things and when put out to the ether all kinds of scenarios can be conjured up through them, so one should, if they can, just think about what thoughts they send to other souls and also what thoughts they think about on a daily basis. All thoughts are received and acted upon. Not necessarily in the context of their asking but in a way that ultimately gives the answer. The world you live in is a very complex place as you know it but take in the universe as you know it and then you are beginning to understand the enormity of the work in the world of spirit, for everything is connected.

Everyone needs a purpose in life but it's to what purpose each soul presents itself that makes the difference to one and all. Some souls need to be in an active environment continually being challenged and worked upon. Whereas others are quite happy to keep a low profile and strive forward in a more gentle way. Others don't seem to mind doing more or less nothing, just letting others take the strain for them until something interests their mind and then they themselves decide to investigate and work in that direction, mainly for their own gratification and satisfaction with no thought of others or contribution towards others. Mankind is a very complex and devious being, more so in the times that surround one at this moment in time. Things have evolved in this way and one shall have to see the outcome of such happenings. The natural side of life in many cases has been eroded from mankind and society simply because of the conditions placed upon one and the order in which each and everyone lives. This does not mean to say that it shall always be so, for mankind has made many adaptations in the history of itself but sadly never heeds what has transferred before and just seems to blunder onwards with no thought of past tense. We have many things to learn in our earthbound lives but recollection it seems never seems to come to the fore in all that we do and attempt to do. We in spirit try our best to rectify this anomaly but it seems to fall on deaf ears.

Blessed are those that seek the Lord for theirs shall be the kingdom of Heaven. Heaven is an apt description for that which lies ahead. It's acceptable to those on the earth plane as is with those within the kingdom of Heaven. Words were put in this terminology for those who at that moment in time needed such understanding to be able to grasp what was being told. Too many nowadays the kingdom of Heaven is 'old hat' as the saying goes. They have flown in planes, gone into space and nothing holds any credibility for them anymore. It's those who have faith in their own convictions that makes the difference from one soul to another. Many forms of religion are steeped in myth expounded by those who in fact are giving the souls guidance at the expense of their own souls, but at the appointed time all things are rectified and put in a clear field of play, so one should not worry over such implications for the outcome is the same for all, likewise choice and decisions are still one's own.

The extremes of man are sometimes more than extreme in the way that others perceive their actions. Every action starts from some archaic action on the part of an individual or individuals. Add prestige and glory into this action and it becomes a ritual that somehow gains momentum through the ages. Man used to kill for the need for food, now it seems he kills just for the fun of it without thought for those he kills. One can guise these barbaric acts in any shape or form but they are barbaric with no thought for those who suffer from its action. Nature is the natural predator in all cases. It's mans intervention in this subject that has altered things making it possible for those who perpetrate such actions. They shall learn eventually but that does not help those animals and birds involved in such actions.

Possessiveness is a trait most souls suffer from. Wanting this and wanting that with no real thought as to why this should be. Evolvement makes such things happen and shall always do so. One sees and has their own examples of what one would like to own, for that in itself is a form of self-preservation, but to many it is just an imaginary dream with no concept of it ever happening, so one should look carefully at what one wants and wishes for. Many souls do reach a point of exactitude but even then they feel that they need more. One can only fill a bottle once without emptying it and it's the same with life itself; we can achieve and amass all kinds of things but at the end of the day can do nothing with them when the final curtain falls. So it's much better to achieve something and savour the experience than try some other venture in a completely different field, for at the end of the day it's only the knowledge and experience that one can take forward. This in itself is very hard to express to many and even harder to explain to others, for what one soul has amassed, another can put asunder in a very short space of time, so go experience things, even attempt things that in the past one thought impossible, for NOTHING is impossible with the right frame of mind. So you see, we do try to coerce one in one way and another, but at the end of the day it's one's own self-will that can make this happen.

Victory is a beautiful word but who needs victory and why? We all wish to be victorious in all we do, so when do we realise that we have become victorious in our achievements? Well, it's when one starts to think of other ventures. We all attempt to set ourselves goals even if in many ways we do not score, but does that matter? The experience of the attempt made us wiser in some aspects of life, giving us an insight towards our next encounter. No one achieves everything that they attempt. Failure is as good as victory, for in both instances one has gained a knowledge that one did not have before. How do you know if you can do it if you do not try in the first place? One has to learn to crawl, then to walk and talk and it is easier for some than others. Well, just take that information as a measuring rod in life's journey. One always has to start at the beginning; one cannot start at the end. Many souls in one's eyes do not seem to achieve anything but is that really true? Do you know that soul's personality and what they want to do and achieve? One cannot rule or judge others in one's own way of thinking for they are your thoughts, so in reality judge yourselves and not others, for you are all your own judge and jury on this pathway of life.

Perfection is not needed or necessary in all one attempts to do for spirit. Who is perfect and what is perfection; and who's to say what is perfect? What one soul thinks is the ultimate in any one kind of scenario, another might think otherwise. Perfection comes from the eye of the beholder, so if what one has done and achieved is to one's own satisfaction that is as near to perfection as one needs to be. We all get satisfaction from the achievements that we reach and this is how it should be. We may criticise the finished product but get great satisfaction in achieving that which we have done. It's just the same when working with and for spirit. Every soul is different in their approach to what they do and attempt to do, so don't go by what others say in the spiritual sense, for they are not you and their guides are not your guides. Notice can be taken from what they say but not to the extent that it should alter one's way of communication with one's own guides and helpers. It takes time and effort to find souls who are compatible with those with whom they work, for in truth it's just an extension of one's own personality and way of thinking for this to be so. These things are brought to fruition and so the work of spirit progresses, hopefully in the correct direction of those concerned.

Persecution of one's mind is not the way forward on the pathway of life. Things are presented to one and all to see the reaction of each and every soul on the subject portrayed. One cannot themselves alter the frailties of the world at large. Religions are as they are and have been this way since time immemorial. They come and go. Man cannot control time but he can contribute towards the downward spiral of nature and all it envelops. One can sit and think on the possibilities that could be brought to bear on such subjects but bringing them to fruition is quite a different matter. Spirit cannot interfere in the fabrics of the universe for everything is relative in ones physical life and also in spirit. Nations and people come and go and man himself has to learn history is there for all to see and understand. But does anybody of consequence ever study these immortal words and bring to the forefront the understanding of such information? No, for mankind has moved on and what applied then does not now at this present time.

Experimentation is what is needed in all aspects of life and if one does not try, how does one expect to know the answers? One is never too old to attempt anything. The human form is exceptional in its make-up, for it has developed to what it is today through experimentation in all kinds of different ways thus bringing one to the point that we are at this moment in time, so whatever one tries to achieve is not a waste of time and effort. One learned from a child to be what one is now, so what's the difference in continuation of this theme? Time and tide wait for no man so go and do what you think or feel you must do for it is only you can find the outcome of doing so. It's up to oneself. One does not have to indulge in such activities if one does not feel one can do such things, so think of what opportunities might be placed in one's pathway and then act as one thinks appropriately. Love life, for that is what it is there for and only you can do it, nobody else, for it's your life.

Exhibitionism is not the way forward in spiritualism. Many souls do fall victim to this way of working simply through their own egotism thus resulting in a mockery of what spirit are trying to portray. Don't get this message wrong, those in spirit like to have humour and laughter in their working with those on the earth plane but to actually bring gestures and the like into messages is not befitting this kind of working. Those who do this find out to their own demise what one should and should not do when working with the spirit realms. We are not staid in our way of working but some spirit find this kind of communication degrading when they have taken the time and effort to come forward to a loved one. This does not mean that spirit will not work with those of this nature but will in time inspire them to a different outlook and way of thinking and working with spirit.

Uncertainty dogs everyone's pathway in life, for that is what life is all about. Nothing is a 'dead cert' as the gambling phrase applies, otherwise what would be the point to life if everything one wanted or did turned out to ones hearts' desire. Nothing in fact would be done for nobody would have to attempt many of the menial tasks that are performed on a day-to-day basis. Uncertainty brings a levelling aspect to ones lives making one think about how to do things and whether one can accomplish that which they would try to do. It may not seem fair to many but that is what life is - a continual battle with oneself, those around one and nature and the elements. Life as such can be easy or hard as to how one applies themselves to that which they feel they have to do.

Questions, questions, always questions, but without questions what would one learn? It is correct to ask questions as long as one understands that the answer is not necessarily given in the context of its asking. Do not be afraid of asking questions. If we who are working with you do not know, there are many who we can ask, for there are all kinds of souls who have information and bring understanding to the questions asked. Life, we have said before, is like a game. It's how you play your part in this game that is of the greatest importance. Do not be shy or afraid of things that one sees or thinks one sees, in that sense go for it no matter what it may be, for you do not know the outcome until you have attempted what you feel you must do, for as we have stressed many times before, winning and losing are just experiences and that is of the greatest importance on this pathway of life.

Blindness to religion is something one will always have to contend with. Each and every soul has their own opinion about God. Is there a God or isn't there a God? Well, that's up to each soul's thoughts on the matter at hand. One cannot prove either side of the case. Arguments can be brought to bear in each and every case to prove their own point, also some souls have been hit some time in their lives, and that makes them bitter towards any kind of God that would relieve them of their loved ones in all kinds of circumstances. That is why it is most difficult to try to attempt to prove that there is a life after life and that God is part of that scenario. In these conditions those souls are left until their time expires and then they see and feel for themselves all that is around them .Then they can make their own assumptions as to what it is all about, but gentle persuasion sometimes makes these souls think about such things, it's then when we in spirit can bring to bear our influence, so not all is lost if the seeds sown in time bring forth enlightenment to those in question. It is still as difficult today to bring enlightenment to souls as it was in times past and we think it shall remain so for quite some time, but discussion on the subject does help in some circumstances as all souls need an answer or somebody or something to blame or explain why these things are allowed to happen.

Some questions received have to be answered by others with a higher understanding of such matters and all these things take time so always have patience with spirit. Everything has to evolve in its own way. Nothing can be brought to the forefront instantaneously. We do answer to the best of our abilities but sometimes it's oneself that is part and parcel of the answer and the question asked, and with time one answers their own question themselves. This being the case we stand back and let one work things out for themselves. So now you understand why answers are not instantaneous. It's your world and it's your life and you yourselves have to live it. 'We have been there and got the tee-shirt' as the saying does and we can only observe, but inspiration can and is sent in all instances of one's life, it's up to each and every individual to interpret that which has been sent in their own way and act accordingly upon their interpretation.

The Lord in His wonderment beseems and receives us all. This is so in the respect that as God is part of us we ourselves are part of God. Not many souls would agree on such a subject but that is their opinion. One cannot dictate faith and religion to anyone. It has been attempted in the past and in most cases has failed miserably. The span of one's time on earth does not, in most cases, give one a true understanding of the evolvement of everything around us, also the impact that mankind is having and has had on the environment. Everything basically is here for a reason even if we don't fully understand the reason at this moment in time. Those on the earth plane now are being awakened to such things but commerce rears its ugly head and devious ones capitalise on such things. We have pointed out before that the earth was made to sustain itself and all that it contained but things themselves are starting to change and that is simply through man's involvement. Mankind's involvement has started to alter the balance in some areas, which is to the detriment of himself and everything else on this earth.

Happiness is thine, sayeth the Lord. Happiness is up to one's own self and how one addresses life itself. One can bring happiness to one's own soul and to others if the circumstances prevail. Happiness is a frame of mind that all can attain if they really wish it. Life brings many trials and tribulations in its living. We only learn by experience and to get experience we have to participate ourselves in all kinds of scenarios for this occurrence to take place. Many try to overcome things by trying not to get involved but that action brings that soul experience in another way, and all in all, experience is gained. Happiness can also be attained in these different circumstances; it's how one adapts themselves to that which is around them. Love life, for life loves you if you will only let it. Love is shown in many examples, it's up to oneself to be able to see and read these signs of love when they are presented. Giving love is quite a simple thing to do and in most cases is reciprocated by the soul the love is sent or given to. Even if one sees no response to ones efforts in this way, not all efforts are wasted. Great things can be achieved through little gestures liken great oaks come from little acorns. So think on happiness and you will become amazed at what you shall find and see by just applying it, happiness is like a rolling snowball, it gets bigger the further it goes.

Worthy is he who worships the Lord our God, for in doing so brings upon himself true love and understanding in this world as it is today. To love God is to love oneself and there is nothing wrong with that, for through loving in that nature helps one to love others and that is a great thing in this day and age. Mankind is moving within itself with communication being eroded from their day to day way of living. One only learns through experience and having a good old NATTER helps each other to get information and understanding. Churches used to play a great part in this activity but this is a diminishing trend. The community spirit needs to be revived again but that is up to each and every individual to play their part in such an enterprise. Situations change all kinds of things on this earth so we shall have to see if some kind of scenario arises to help adjust this form of communication again. One-to-one is a good way of being shown and taught but this is difficult in this day and age. In past times the elderly still lived with their children if they had any and were a useful form of information for the young ones to tap into. Today's trend seems to shun this style and way of living through the pressures of today's standard of living. Nothing stays the same, for everything has to evolve but it's how things evolve that makes the difference to us all.

The mineral deposits that are in this world are there to be used but used in a way that in itself does not desecrate the natural side and animal side at that location. One has seen by past examples how nature itself can relocate itself if left to its own devises. This should be so in these areas where this kind of enterprise has taken place and not, in most cases, use this land for other purposes. Mankind itself can live in most environments but not so with the animals and natural side of the equation. Nature and the animal side of life can look after itself if left in an environment that is suited to their needs but this is not the case in most instances, for those with money always need to make more money. This is not a sin in itself, for in past times it has benefitted mankind greatly but some souls do not seem to be able to say enough is enough. It seems to become an addiction to them and the way that they live and think. Man and mankind is just a terminology but this in itself encompasses the female gender as well. All this writing about all things is 'all well and good' one might say when seen from afar, and "who am I" one might say "to do anything about such things"? Well my friend, these writings are of great importance to anyone in a position to do anything about them and like most things that starts from new, has to make new inroads on that subject but if one has already been given certain examples it makes it all the easier to act upon. Not that many would take notice but with a repertoire of such magnitude one has much to fall back upon and rectify their understanding on such subjects.

Consideration for others is a useful tool when working with and for spirit. Everybody can find fault in one thing and another. The secret is to be able to see these faults and not aggravate them. Gentle persuasion with consideration helps in all cases as one will find out if one tries to apply this kind of approach. One can do many things for many souls if one just took the time and effort to do so, but who says one should do these things? Well, to start with, one's inner self can be used as a guide but one has to be able to reach one's inner self to make this kind of working available to oneself. Meditation is a good way of reaching one's inner self but one must do this with a closed but open mind. Closed to that which is around them and thoughts that one tends to mull over, but open to one's inner self if one can attain that level of communication and relaxation. There are many ways of trying to attain this form of communication, it's up to oneself to try and see what suits one best.

There is always time for deliberation in anything that one wants or needs to do. He who thinks first does not have to think last. This may be case in question to oneself, for the more one listens the more one understands and learns. This has applied many times when younger but the truth of the matter is did one remember what these souls told you for your own benefit? For many they are quite happy in their day-to-day experiences and seek no further input to their daily lives because this is how they have always been but when one becomes affected by spirit and the knowledge of spirit everything takes on a different meaning and this in turn makes for one to start to seek more information on the subject. As in your case you feel you need to know more about the religions of the world as they are today. It also would be handy if one could find out more about those religions that have gone into obscurity. Well, there is nothing wrong in any of these thinking's and one might think why does one have these thoughts at this moment in time. We ourselves understand your thirst for knowledge of the past and might be guilty in that vein of thought.

Patience Strong was the name given to a person but patience and strong read either way makes for good evidence as to what and how one should be on this pathway of life. One needs patience in most things that one undertakes and combined with strength make one a formidable person in that which one wishes and needs to do or accomplish. Everything starts from nothing, it's how one develops this nothing that makes the difference to us all. To try things that seem impossible or irrelevant can give one a good insight to oneself. Never be afraid of making a mistake. We all make mistakes in one way or another and hopefully through making such mistakes one learns and accrues knowledge for the next encounter in a similar vein, so you see, nothing is wasted – even failure. Knowledge has been accrued in that field and one tries not to go down that same road again should the occasion arise. Life is good, life is strange. We all have to live our lives no matter how long or short it may be.

Well my son, we sit and write again. I use the word 'son' as we are all sons and daughters, brothers and sisters in the world of spirit and that is what you are now in contact with. Others may decry you as to whether this is true or not, but can they themselves contact the world of spirit in this way? Everyone works with and for spirit in a different way, so who's to say what's right and wrong? For we proclaim that anyone who works with and for spirit should and shall be blessed. One may wonder as to why one had never been aware of spirit until one had grown old. Well you have always been aware in your dreams or nightmares but could not understand the underlying thread to it all. We work with you in this way to help us in spirit to advance those who wish to work in this capacity for the benefit of mankind and spirit. The saying 'you get your reward in Heaven' is true but that does not mean to say you cannot be rewarded whilst in the physical, but you shall have to leave that for us to decide in which avenue this shall be given.

Discernability is often brought into play when working with and for spirit. Not everything is clear cut from spirit but it is. It's the interpretation or discern ability to understand that makes the difference from one soul to another. Messages, one might say, are not clear cut but that's only through the understanding of the soul receiving the message. We are not here to live your lives or direct you to do this or that, for you are your lives and you have to do what you feel you must do. It's rather like a play when one is acting - we are just in the wings ready to give one a prompt should one need one.

Victorious shall be the work of those in spirit. Victorious in the sense that those on the earth plane shall finally have the choice of learning about the world of spirit and all that it appertains to. Every soul has to have something to believe in and spirit hopefully shall be able to give them this belief. Each soul is an individual and has their own thoughts and impressions on any given subject but with the knowledge of life after death shall make a great impact upon each and every soul to whom this knowledge is available. Everything has to have a starting place and spirit in themselves are agreed that the time is fast approaching for this knowledge to be forthcoming.

He who believeth in Him shall not perish. A wording of old but with the same emphasis as when first written, it's only the wording that has changed through time. The message is still the same, even if at times it's too hard to comprehend the truth of such writings in today's society with all the technology that surrounds one. As the saying goes 'there is never smoke without fire' and this can and has to be applied to the writings and teachings of what is called *the Gospel to our Lord God*. Many things can and have been proven in today's society and this is a case in point. Who or what does one believe for there are so many different religions? Now that is where there's no smoke without fire and the fire itself is your Lord God in as much as you want to define it. After that it's one's own conscience that comes into play and that's the example that one finds one should follow. Death comes to us all in the physical sense, that is inevitable but it's the after death side to it all that brings the most controversy in all religions. This does not matter for we are all different, but to bring God into the equation that one soul must kill another soul in and through the named God is inadmissible.

When shall the word of God truly be known? It is now but not in the true sense. With time comes change and with change comes new revelations although these revelations in themselves have meaning, they do not reflect the true wishes of our Lord our God in as much as the continual conflict amongst one's different nations and races, creeds and breeds. As one understands, one religion cannot be understood by all asunder but the underlying theme to it all should be one of love and harmony not one of hate and destruction. As history has proved itself, it's taken generations for mankind to get to the position it now stands at, but has it truly learned anything in the spiritual sense of things? It's with love, compassion and understanding that spirit come forth to bring mankind a greater understanding of itself and all that life itself contains. We fervently need mankind's appraisal of spirit, for to love life is to love one another and this has to be made possible for the continuation of the species.

The word of your Lord God is told in many ways, for it's through each and every individuals' thoughts and writings on such matters that brings us to the conclusions that we have today. In the beginning there was God. Afterwards we have spirit and all that that entails. But who is God? In reality has anyone ever met Him? Questions many might ask and questions many might answer in their own interpretation. When mankind goes to war with one another they all ask God to help them defeat the opposing side. How can God help when He Himself is the divine being that they both worship? The answer is the side that is the strongest, for man himself brought about such conflicts in the first place not God and in doing so they must look to their own involvement of the situation and not try to blame God when things don't go as they would like them to. It's a strange and wonderful world that one lives upon and in being so brings within itself all kinds of scenarios that mankind and everything else that dwells upon and within has to contend with.

What faith dost thou have in the Lord your God? Many have been asked such a question and many answers have been given but what is your interpretation of your Lord God? How does He Himself fit into your mind's eye? Yes, God is part and parcel of everything but does that seem right when some things in your way of thinking are wrong and should not be allowed. This has always been the case with mankind for who's to say what is right and what is wrong? It's always been through consensus of thought and discussion that brings one to an answer to the question asked. This in itself is correct but some souls through the treatment and environment that they have been brought up in have different thoughts so how does one equate those circumstances simply by time itself, for time reveals all to all but that is not what the consensus of those on the earth plane want, so laws are established and souls are made to abide by those laws be they bad or good. We live a life which we gain both experience and knowledge that in some circumstances may be passed to others for the good of the whole, but life itself has not altered over generations of time in the way we see others and how we react to others, so getting everyone to have a common denomination in their way of thought and being is a challenge that spirit themselves are embroiled with.

Divisions in life come in many sections and many ways. What's suitable for one is not necessarily suitable for another. One makes life itself on a day-to-day basis and it's how one fits into this daily stream of life that makes one the person that they are. Everyone has choice to a certain degree and can 'alter their lot' (as the saying goes) in many instances. It's knowing how and when to change.

There are many references to all kinds of religious happenings but sadly the reading of these writings is more or less impossible due to the fact that those who cherish such information do not wish others to witness it due to the content of such writings might bring reflection upon their own religious beliefs thus causing consternation amongst its converts. Many ancient examples have been destroyed over eons of time and most of what is left is of a nature of the writers' own interpretation, but even in those writings there is a grain of truth about the whole episode that has been capsulated, so if one is fortunate to be able to see and read such that is left, make one's own interpretation of what it tries to say and mean to one themselves. The Lord giveth and the Lord taketh. Glory be to the Lord our God. And who is God? It's all within the eye of the beholder and hopefully this in itself brings help and uniformity to those concerned.

'Everything comes to he who waits' as the saying goes, but in some instances the waiting can be minimised through one's own intervention. 'Time and tide wait for no man', another saying with truth. It's the application of these wordings and sayings that plays the important part of our lives. Many things happen in this journey through life; some would say good, others would say bad, but nothing lasts forever especially if one themselves makes a conscious effort to alter ones circumstances at any given time. Each and every individual are the perpetrators of their own destiny but to understand such things often comes at a time when life itself is coming to a conclusion. They say 'with age comes knowledge', and this in itself is true but if one does not realise that knowledge and partakes and uses it to their and others' advantage, what was the point of learning it in the first place? Many souls learn many things and never realise what knowledge they have received simply because they think in their own minds that everybody should know that too and never try to pass on to other individuals who would benefit. Everybody and everything learns through trial and error, it's the understanding of what one has learned that is of the greatest importance and how one can apply that knowledge to others no so gifted.

Cause and effect have a very true and positive effect on one's everyday life. Nobody can live the perfect life, for the obstacles that are placed upon one's pathway of life are there for a very good reason and one themselves are perpetrators of many of these obstacles themselves. Nobody's perfect. One in one's own minds eye might think others perfect but we all have skeletons in our cupboards. That is true; it's the understanding of what these skeletons mean and how they arrived is the secret to their understanding. Life is complicated. If it was not, one would soon become bored but all kinds of different scenarios make the living of one's life quite exciting. We cannot all be philosophers on this pathway of life but with guidance can help others to try and understand what life itself is truly all about.

Decisions, always decisions, but the enormity of the decisions is what makes us who and what we are. All through one's life one has to make decisions without knowing the consequences, but without such, life itself would be pretty dull. One thinks of many things on one's pathway of life and wonders if one could or should do this or that. Well, the only answer to that question is to do or try to do whatever appeals to one at any given time, for time itself is of the essence in any situation so what's the point of waiting and wondering about such things when in fact one could try. It's just a matter of trying in most cases. The old adage of 'nothing ventured nothing gained' is quite true. Everybody has goals that, in their mind, might sound as fantasies but in truth could and should be played out, so don't just wonder about such things, have a go. So next time one feels attracted to do something then do it, for nobody else can do it for you and at the end of the day, it's your life and your thoughts so put them into practice. Diverse ability is a wondrous thing so just go with the flow and see what arises from doing so. So what's stopping you from doing or trying to? Only your own self confidence.

The conscious and the subconscious are two tools available to spirit and mankind itself to administer certain criteria to the human mind. As one understands, one is one's own judge and jury, so what are the criteria that one judges oneself upon? Only that which one feels just in one's own mind at any given time. How we obtain this feeling of just is through the living of one's life on the earth plane and all that it throws and shows us during this time. We all have to learn for that's what life is all about even if others would totally disagree, and by learn we mean in a positive way, not solely beneficial as most souls think is the true way forward. Things may seem different from times past but the same problems still raise their ugly heads, only in differing circumstances as the environment that surrounds one allows. Not everyone can learn everything, for the stage is too vast for anyone to incorporate all that needs to be known and on the other side of the coin one themselves have to experience such things to enable them to truly understand that which they have learned. Many gain vast knowledge through the reading from books and that in itself is not bad, for that's what books are for but without a mind capable of assimilating all this knowledge, what does one truly gain through doing so? Things one does on a physical basis is a good example to go by, for if one has done a thing one truly know what and how that was achieved. It may sound trivial writing such words that truly one already knows about but others on this earth plane may find it enlightening.

Quiet is the soul at rest, when the sun is in the west

It's the time that we like best; for all that we might behest

About the world one wishes to know, as along ones pathway one must go

to see the sights that one must see, if only you would think of me,

The one who's with you through and through, helping with the things that you must do

To find this place you want so much, that you can feel but cannot touch.

It's there within you you will find, if you could listen to your mind;

A mind that's full of things to do, when we try to contact you

So sit and wait and you will see, just how easy it all shall be.

It's been done before as you do know, so sit and wait for things to flow

From us to you as in a dream, for when we come we do not scream

The things we wish you to attain, and for the knowledge you need to gain

At making contact with us all, for we will never let you fall

Into the pit of sheer despair, for we are always here for you to care.

It's your life that you have to live, and of our love we wish to give

To help you on this road you pass, so of our thoughts you can amass

To help you with your daily life, and keep you always free from strife.

The Lord giveth and the Lord taketh and so it shall always be. Every soul has a span on the earth plane according to that which they need to know and experience. Some may take this as not a thing that any God would do but it is decided by the soul themselves as to what they need to do whilst on the earth plane also how long they wish to stay for whatever experience they need to gain and the knowledge that goes with it so you see everything is for a reason – a reason that is most complex in many instances.

Many things are positioned on life's pathway simply to see ones reaction to them and ones response to them. This in itself can come in any shape or form; a continuing variety of sights, sounds and smells. One may not agree with this philosophy but time shall prove it to those aware of the world of spirit. We do not mean to say that life itself is self-governed by spirit but they do have occasion to inspire and sometimes cajole one into a different train of thought or deed. One does not realise this as one's own imagination plays the greater part in all that one experiences on a day to day basis. So one is one's own person and not controlled by any other outward force. It's all down to inspiration and how one interprets such inspiration sent. One can find inspiration in the most obscure thing and from such observation great knowledge can be obtained. Many things in life are found or discovered in this way. It's the application of the soul who sees and understands that makes the difference to one and all.

We all have the power of imagination and creativity and the two put together can make for all kinds of scenarios so take life as it comes and as you live your life seek and you shall find but it's up to oneself what one seeks and how and when one shall find that which they seek. Live life, love life, for life certainly loves you. It's only ones own selfish outlook on certain things that brings about some of the conditions that are placed upon one.

Each and every nation has had words thrown upon them and not always to ridicule. People themselves are given the terminology of nicknames but do they themselves go to court to have such names eradicated? No. So why should such pompass beings as of today be allowed to say that this and that is not ethical in the terminology that it is given. Many souls use certain circumstances to endeavour to make themselves be elevated in the eyes of the masses, but by doing so bring condemnation from others. Common sense should prevail in most of these instances but life being as it is at this moment in time one just seems to have to obey the rules. We all tend to be ruled by rules of one nature or another and it's mankind itself who make such rules. Many rules seem to last an eternity whereas others disappear with the passing of time. As one lives one's life look more closely at what is happening and one will be surprised at what one might glean from such observations. One does not have to be a professor to do these things just a general observation is all that is needed.

The life that lives is the life that dies for one in spirit does not live a life as on the physical plane for one has lost one's physical body and have become spirit themselves. This part of the explanation is left to be experienced by each and every soul who passes to the spiritual side of life for only then can one fully understand the implications of one's transition and the experience gained through doing so.

www.ingramcontent.com/pod-product-compliance
Ingram Content Group UK Ltd.
Pitfield, Milton Keynes, MK11 3LW, UK
UKHW020225250726
13967UKWH00001B/190